CEO-LED SALES

THE NEW MODEL TO TRANSFORM YOUR BUSINESS

CEO-LED SALES

THE NEW MODEL TO TRANSFORM YOUR BUSINESS

ANDREW PHILLIPS

Social Star

2/218 Lower Plenty Road, Rosanna, Vic, 3084

Published by Social Star 2021

Typeset in Raleway by Working Type Studios

Printed in Australia by IngramSpark, part of the Ingram Content Group.

Hardback ISBN 978-0-6450386-0-6

Paperback ISBN 978-0-6450386-1-3

eBook ISBN 978-0-6450386-2-0

Catalogue records for this book are available from the National Library of Australia

A catalogue record for this book is available from the National Library of Australia

Social Star ☆
Publishing

socialstar.com.au

To my daughter, Clair, whose never-failing strength
and clarity of thought started me on this journey.

'Andrew is all about results. Using his natural forensic ability, he uncovers and develops opportunities across his team.'
— **John Preller, Head of Public Sector, Qualtrics (ANZ)**

'If a sales relationship characterised by integrity, intelligence, empathy and respect is something you aspire to, you should listen to Andrew. He knows what he's talking about.'
— **Michael Vanderheide, ex CEO of Cenitex**

'Andrew's approach to sales strategy is refreshing. He has the vision of the outcomes and the drivers for success through all stages of a deal, from the approach to pursue, respond, and ultimately into negotiations through to closing.'
— **Greg Thomas, Senior Solutions Executive, Unisys**

Contents

Foreword

My sales journey started in a local camera shop as I paid my way through university. I was lucky enough to work for someone who believed that sales is a process that should be taught, that there were basic rules and skills that needed to be learned and honed, just like chess. Unlike chess, there was never a winner and loser, but an outcome where the customer bought the camera they needed, and the salesperson maintained a *customer for life*. My early mentor taught me two other important lessons: you need sales to pay the bills; customers know lots of people so referrals are the best advertising.

After university my first job was, what Andrew Phillips refers to, as a 'box dropper' in medium enterprise and the public sector. This taught me a lot about the complexity of selling technology in B2B (Business-to-Business) transactions. Over time, my sales journey evolved and grew to selling complex B2B technology infrastructure solutions.

I met Andrew in the mid 2000s when I was incubating a managed-services business with a large global systems integrator, which over 10 years grew into a very large global business focusing on large multi-year contracts across 14 countries. During that time, Andrew and I worked together on several large deals. As with all good sales-people, we won some, we lost some, and took lessons from every deal we were involved in.

This experience taught me that some CEOs and senior executives did not come from a sales background, and even those with a sales background, didn't understand the difference between selling high-volume transactional deals and big complex deals. Many of the things they implemented as best practice to run their sales teams did not work in big-complex-deal teams. What was worse, when you questioned these assumptions and practices, you were seen to be challenging the status quo and threatening the hierarchy.

However, a key lesson I learned is that questioning and challenging is what disruptors do. They question the status quo and ask why things are done certain ways and look for a different way. A better way. As a fellow disruptor, Andrew openly questions the status quo. He points to great examples of the structures, assumptions and metrics that traditional sales teams are built upon that don't work in B2B-complex-deal selling.

For those of us who have lived and breathed large-complex-B2B deals, we know that metrics, such as the pipeline being 3:1, don't work for big-complex-deal hunting. Personally, it worked fine when I was managing a high-volume box-dropping sales team, but not as I moved into large complex deals. Individual quotas and territories were created for travelling salespeople in the typewriter business, yet today we still hold on to that as the way it's done. With all the money invested in CRM (Customer Relationship Management) systems, we still have sales managers who believe their job is to administer the pipeline. Andrew points out many of these issues and highlights many things that people, who have had successful careers selling big-complex-B2B-solutions-and-services deals, know to be true.

Andrew's comments about heroes and the hero sales team get to the heart of some of the issues in complex-deal sales. This is a team sport where CEOs and Senior Executives are part of the on-field leadership team. Imagine a professional sporting team where the Head Coach and Club President did not go to the games, but simply had the team Captain send them the results and probability of winning next week. As a team sport, selling culture must start at the top of the organisation. The organisation must also be structured for success; everyone must understand their role and be remunerated accordingly.

Every organisation needs a plan for how they will succeed. As my early mentor taught me, getting sales right is critical, without it nothing else really matters. If the organisation you lead decides to go after big-complex-B2B-solution-and-services deals, then you need a plan to succeed in a space that is highly competitive and always changing due to the rapidly changing nature of the digital landscape. *CEO-Led Sales* provides great insight and ideas that I highly recommend you take time to explore in developing that plan.

David D'Aprano, Principal, D2&Associates Pty Ltd,
November 2020

Introduction

I am very lucky to have accumulated experience from a wide variety of jobs across my working life. I've been a motor mechanic, a policeman, a small-business owner operating two scuba-diving schools and a commercial diving business in NSW and ACT, an enterprise sales executive, a global IT company executive and a strategic advisor. This breadth of experience has taught me a lot.

I left school early and started my working life as a motor mechanic. I'd always had a passion for pulling things apart and either fixing them or making them better. And although I liked the work, I soon realised that this wasn't the life-long career for me, so I went back and finished my schooling.

My next career was in the police force where I had a wide range of training and experience: police diving, search and rescue, road accident rescue, special operations, witness protection, bomb search, fraud and task forces, and general policing in the ACT and Christmas Island. The diversity of skills I learnt from this wide range of policing roles and the required discipline of those years have been instrumental in formulating the person I am today.

My parents were a big influence early in my life. They taught me to work hard, which is a bit of a cliché because I think everyone's parents try to teach this lesson. My dad did it by example. There was no job that he would not turn his hand to on our property, from farming worms to building a stone house or repairing an old steam engine, and everything else in between. He created within me a mindset of 'just get the job done' and the confidence to do anything, to not just focus on the skills you have but to look beyond them. He encouraged me to take a long-term view of a problem and focus not on the problem, but on the outcome. My mum is a skilled spinner and weaver, and she taught me that often what you need isn't available so you have to make it from scratch, using your creativity to produce something beautiful.

The most significant aspect of my life that has taught me about this long-term/outcome-focused view was bringing my daughter up after her mother passed away. My daughter was 15 years old and dealing with the immediate overwhelming grief was critical. Equally importantly, I found was putting strategies in place for what I termed 'self-rescue'. We spent a lot of time understanding how to navigate each day to arrive at the end of it with a good outcome, even though there may have been some emotional events along the way.

The key was that if we found ourselves in a circumstance that was overwhelming, the question was: 'How can we "self-rescue"?' After the first three to four months, I no longer worried about the day-to-day. I focused instead on what the outcome was going to be. What was the best long-term result for my daughter when she turned, say, 18 or 24 or 28? What could my daughter be and achieve over that time? I kept that long-term focus, playing the infinite game was front of my mind, and that has certainly seen her develop into a fantastic individual. Clair is forging strongly ahead in her career and is married to a great bloke.

You might be surprised to hear that my biggest lesson in selling was my time as a sworn officer in the Australian Federal Police. I've explained this to people many times, that being a good police officer is all about being able to sell someone the benefits of telling the truth. It is about talking to a mix of people, from a Hong Kong-based heroin importer to the Commander of a US nuclear-powered submarine, in a way that makes them feel comfortable enough to tell you what you need to find out, generally under some of the most adverse conditions for communication possible. It is about asking the right questions to move to the next stage in the process, which requires on-the-spot critical thinking, analysis, reasoning and dealing with ambiguity.

Essentially, that's what a good salesperson does. They take into account a lot of information, analyse it, remove the noise, and bring back the essential things in an ordered fashion that delivers an outcome. A good police officer can do this. I call it using a forensic approach.

Looking back, I realise that my entire working life has been about selling. Regardless of the role, it comes down to knowing your discipline exceptionally well, engaging with your audience, listening, creating questions that move you forward, and listening some more. I'm passionate about taking a genuine interest in people and delivering an outcome that is second to none. I also, by the way, love being sold to. I've never been able to resist a good sales pitch.

I've written this book for the CEO who is at a transition point in their role. You may have missed the number for a year or two, you may be new in the position and feel the need to transform, or perhaps you're just tired of the excuses and missed opportunities from the sales team. I've written this book for the CEO who has the energy, focus and drive to implement a profound cultural change in their organisation over a multi-year period.

CEO-Led Sales is an approach that is innovative and different. It doesn't have the old clichés of: 'We will work harder, we will be smarter, we will only pursue the deals we have a chance of winning, we will target new markets, and we will hire better salespeople.' These are relevant things, but they won't work unless you build a new organisation and culture from the ground up.

If you don't build from the ground up, then the same issues and behaviours will filter back in. You'll be planning to have a plan, or you'll have a plan that isn't executed. I've got a favourite saying: 'When you don't know what to do, you do what you know.' I hear people say they have 20 years' worth of experience in XYZ industry, when often all they actually have is one year's experience repeated 20 times over.

I will begin this book by looking at the IT sales environment today, how it has evolved and continues to evolve. I'll then look at the IT sales organisation and how it is currently approaching that sales environment. I'll also look at the immense challenges that CEOs face today. I'll then propose a model that I've created called The Right Model that I believe will help CEOs better align their sales organisation to the sales environment of today and into the future.

And although I predominantly talk about the IT industry, I believe the principles I discuss in this book can be tailored to suit a broad range of organisations (private companies, public-sector corporations, not-for-profits) in many other industries, from heavy or large-scale undertakings — say, building a ship or an airport — to fast-moving consumer goods and everything else in between.

PART A:
THE ENVIRONMENT

In 2006, after working in a number of sales leadership roles in IT organisations, I secured my first job as the overall leader running the ACT branch of a large systems integrator. This was the first time I had full 'Profit and Loss' responsibility. It was the first time I had the responsibility for everyone in the entire branch, from the person that greeted you when you walked in the door, to the person handling the legal requirements, to the person handling the solutions, to the person delivering the actual service, and everyone else in between.

Whilst not all of these people reported directly to me, I was responsible for ensuring the success of the branch and thereby responsible for all of these people's jobs. Our branch was doing about $43 million dollars a year, and shortly after I took over the branch, we lost a major piece of business that took about $20 million out.

So there I was, relatively new in the business, having taken over a business that was healthy at $43 million, then overnight I'm down to $23 million and I've got the same number of staff. I remember it was gut-wrenching. It was one of those moments where I had a cold shiver run through me and I was asking myself over and over: 'What's just happened? I'm new to the company, and I've lost this deal. How can we recover from that?'

I knew immediately I had to take responsibility to turn it around, to ensure the future and ongoing success of the branch, and I told everyone we wouldn't be losing any staff as a result of this.

So what did I do?

I went back to what I knew. What I had previously learned as a police officer and a dive-store manager and from my early days in selling. That if everyone is focused on what their customers need to achieve, then we will deliver better service, leading to our customers being more successful, and if our customers are more successful, then we will also be successful.

Did it work?

I'll come to that later ...

1. Our Clients

Our clients don't wake up in the morning like they did, say, 15 years ago and announce: 'Today I want to buy four X-frame servers' or 'Today I want to buy the latest release of a particular software package.' They wake up in the morning, and they say something like: 'My CEO has told me that we need to acquire a new insurance company', or 'My CEO has told me that we need to open offices in Asia', or 'My CEO has told me we need to increase our clients' success.'

Our clients come to market for outcomes like these and they pass on the entire responsibility for those outcomes to us, the vendor. We are trusted with helping them change and transform their business. The bottom line is our clients are buying infrastructure or pieces of equipment or software less and less; more often they are buying solutions and outcomes. And even when they write 'We want to buy four X-frame servers' or 'We want the latest release of a particular software package' in the tender, they are really looking for those solutions and outcomes. And these solutions and outcomes cannot be delivered if we, the vendor, don't understand the industry our clients are in and where their organisation sits within that industry.

Our Clients Expect Us to Know Their Industry

All organisations today, regardless of what industry they're in, operate in an organisational ecosystem comprising at least four component ecosystems:

Organisational Ecosystem

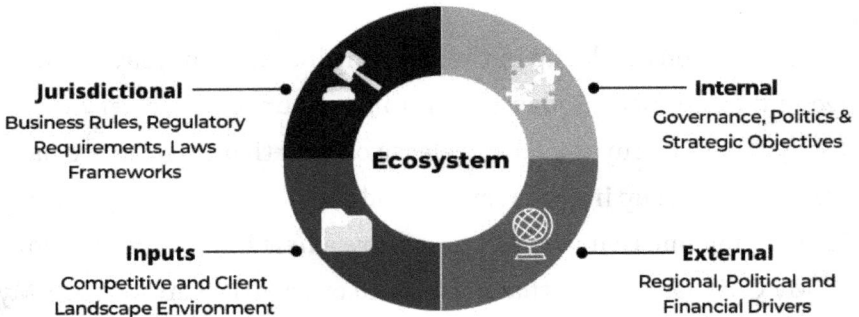

Jurisdictional — Business Rules, Regulatory Requirements, Laws Frameworks

Internal — Governance, Politics & Strategic Objectives

Ecosystem

Inputs — Competitive and Client Landscape Environment

External — Regional, Political and Financial Drivers

Firstly, they operate in the ecosystem of themselves (**internal**). This includes internal governances and processes, politics and strategic objectives within the organisation. It also includes any mergers or acquisitions that are going on in their particular space. Some organisations might appear the same on the outside, but internally they operate in many different ways — they are a complex matrix of formal and informal decision-making processes with key decision-makers throughout their structure.

Secondly, they operate in a competitive and client landscape against similar organisations doing similar things, all vying to win a finite client base (**inputs**). I say 'finite' because I subscribe to the fundamental premise that there are no new clients and that most industries are mature. Of course, there are disruptive organisations like Uber or Airbnb, but these are more the exception than the rule.

Thirdly, there's a legislative ecosystem which includes business rules, regulatory requirements, laws and frameworks that wrap around the entire industry (**jurisdictional**). This is a level playing field of corporate compliance whether it be reporting, or statements of building, or occupational health and safety legislation. For example, many organisations that operate in Australia today are still affected by European privacy legislation and American governance around accounting standards.

Fourthly, and finally, there's the geopolitical and financial ecosystem that includes regional, political and financial drivers (**external**). This layer essentially includes things that fall outside the organisation's control and covers regionality and the global perspective. For example: if a tier-two bank in Singapore goes broke, and my client is a tier-one bank in Australia, then what would the implications be for my client?

These component ecosystems combine to form the overall organisational ecosystem that the CEO or COO faces every single morning. When they read in the newspaper that the American President is either friendly with the Chinese, or not friendly with the Chinese, or friendly with the Russians, or not friendly with the Russians, then this has an effect on how their organisation operates in those markets. They need us, their vendors, to understand how these factors will affect the solution they are looking for.

For example, I was recently involved in a deal with a client who had allowed their infrastructure to age over time as they were unable to get the budget to upgrade it. As a result, they had a requirement they took to market. It was a pretty bland requirement for some cloud, some cloud on their own premises, some cloud in the public domain, some technology to run and manage that cloud, and a little bit of networking kit.

I looked at that requirement and I realised very quickly that what they were really asking for was a major cybersecurity program. This is a combination of the legislative and internal ecosystems. The only reason I knew this was because I was a student of the industry, committed to gathering all the information I could about that industry. I'd read an article in a newspaper a year earlier that reported this organisation had had a major security breach. This breach was reported as a major embarrassment for Australia.

My team and I responded to this organisation's requirement through the lens of the events that happened to them earlier. We responded to that major security breach. We said directly: 'This isn't an upgrade; this is a fundamental cybersecurity program to regain the reputation of Australia and its allies in this particular industry area.'

That's the overriding theme we ran at the tender response and every time we went in to present or to meet with this client. It was a long process over twelve months, so we were able to refine this cyberse-curity theme. Most organisations see security as a technology or a process, which means anyone can deliver it. We took the approach that security is an outcome, supported by technology and processes and people, which is unique because we were then able to shape and own that outcome.

We needed the client to understand that security is there to enable the business, that it isn't a brick wall that stops things from happening. At the time, I had to do a lot of work to convince my team to forget about the technical requirements and sell to the cybersecurity business requirement. We would run briefing sessions every morning, prior to going into the client to be certain that everyone understood how to interpret what they had written from a technical requirement and to ensure they could speak to it fluently in a cybersecurity-business-outcome conversation.

We also ran debriefing sessions afterwards, because it was important to understand that it wasn't good enough just to say the right words. Anybody can do that. Everyone on my team had to be in tune with exactly what the client needed to do to achieve their outcomes and be able to articulate it. And if they weren't able to do so, then I left them behind and they didn't attend the meeting.

Now I guarantee that our competitors responded to the technology requirements equally as well as we did, but they didn't articulate it back to the ecosystems the client was operating within. In the end, we won the deal because we showed the client that we clearly understood their industry and their business. We understood the pain they were going through.

The important thing that comes from this example is you've got to be a student of the industry at all times. You've got to ask yourself every time you see a requirement: 'What do I know about this?', 'What is the backstory?' And if you don't know anything, then Google it — now.

I see this as the whole team's responsibility. It's that important. When, as a team, you understand the pressures the client is under in their marketplace, you become absolutely unique to them. Your conversations with them change. You are still talking about technology, but the client immediately feels that because you know the topic, you are going to be able to do the job better for them.

So what's the best way to illustrate to a new client that you understand their industry? For me, it begins with storytelling. You've got to very descriptively say: 'I understand what's going on locally and regionally. Here are some of the pressures I know about. Are you seeing these same pressures in your environment?' This has to be a collaborative approach. It's not about saying: 'Well, I know you've got this and I know you've got that.' You have to tell a story.

For example, you could say something like: 'We worked with an organisation in New Zealand that was in the same industry as you and they were finding these issues ... Are these some of the issues you are finding?' Instantly, you're describing the same pains that your client is facing, illustrating the same pressures they're under and you've shown them that you've worked on these before, that you can deliver.

You can't just make things up. Your storytelling must be based on facts and everyone on the team has to be on board. Everyone has to understand. An example of this was a recent public-sector opportunity with a state government agency that deals with family services. It came up following a Royal Commission into children in need of care. The Commission report came out with a number of recommendations around how reporting needs to be shared between different agencies within the state government and the wider national organisations. There was a publicly available memorandum of understanding between the state, federal and local governments about how and what data would be shared. This might sound obvious, but you have to read this document and ask, 'How does this affect my client?' Before you go in and meet them.

Coincidentally, in this case, we had worked on a similar opportunity in the US, so we were able to honestly say that we had seen these issues before. We were able to share how we solved the problems in the US and describe the outcomes. We asked the question: 'Is this the sort of thing that you're looking to achieve from the perspective of the recommendations of the Royal Commission?'

We were able to contextualise and convey to the client that we had done the job somewhere else, that we understood the industry and knew their business. I knew for a fact that some of our competitors were talking about speeds and feeds in the cloud. About how well the application would run, or how it would be set up on a person's laptop. Essentially, about how they had the best app. Now, you've still got to have the best app, but you've also got to move beyond that, so you can have better quality conversations with the client to hear a deeper level of the pain that they're facing. Only then can you truly illustrate that you understand and can deliver the solution fully.

I have this equation:

Knowledge + Trust = Credibility.

If you're knowledgeable and your client trusts what you say, then you become credible. When you're credible, you're the first person they'll come to.

If you're trustworthy but you haven't got knowledge, you're not credible. The client won't come to you. If you've got knowledge and you aren't trustworthy, you're not credible. The client won't come to you. You need both. They go hand in hand.

Showing your client that you're knowledgeable is the first step and comes through conversation and storytelling. Trust is the second step and is built by delivering everything that you say you're going to deliver. Everyone gives people a level of trust when they first meet. If you're making stuff up about the industry, then you're not showing knowledge and there's no chance to build trust. You're out the door. If you've illustrated knowledge and you're doing exactly what you said you were going to do, then you've built credibility.

Let me give a small, everyday example of this. In this case, I'm the client. I recently went out to purchase a new smartwatch. I went into a store, stated my intention and the salesperson immediately replied, 'Great, what's your lifestyle like?' I answered that I was a runner and a mountain biker who likes swimming and does a bit of rowing. Then she asked, 'What types of activities do you do?' I talked about the activities I do. I talked more about mountain-bike riding. I talked about running, about kayaking, about paddleboarding and hiking. I talked about all these activities and she could have at this point said, 'Okay. Great. This particular watch suits all these activities. There you go. Thank you very much.'

But she wanted to dive in further, so she asked me, 'Do you do these activities remotely? Do you travel for these activities? Do you do any of these activities in hostile environments?' She kept asking me questions to prove to me that she was interested in what my outcomes were. She was also proving to me that she knew the capabilities of all these watches before she marched me over to the watch aisle.

So by the time we did march over to the watch aisle, we came to a very natural outcome. I had someone who had asked me a lot of meaningful and relevant questions to build knowledge and gain my trust, which led to her seeming credible to me. As a result, I was happy to take her recommendation straight off. And, unsurprisingly, when she asked, 'Would you like some extra warranty on that?' I was happy to be up-sold at the same time.

Now you might say that this example isn't relevant to multimillion-dollar deals. Of course it's different, but the fundamentals are the same, it just happens in a quicker, more contained way. Obviously, the salesperson in this example couldn't have been a student of mine, but she was able to acquire the required knowledge quickly by asking questions and the rest followed.

They didn't try to build a relationship with me. That's a word I won't be using in any methodology in this book: 'relationships'. I don't use that word. I just don't think it's relevant in the sales process. I think we all need to be really careful when we hear salespeople say, 'I've got a good relationship with X ...' What does that really mean? Does that mean X likes them, and they like X? Is this even relevant?

'Credibility' is the word we need to listen for. That's the word that makes you valuable to your client. I didn't like or dislike the smart-watch salesperson. I didn't have a relationship with her. She built credibility with me, so I followed her on the journey. Now if she had tried to build a relationship — to try to get me to like her — then that's a different emotion altogether. I think 'like' is a very fickle state. We've all liked and disliked people over our lives. Whereas, if people are credible, they maintain that credibility over time, as long as they remain knowledgeable and trustworthy.

Two things you don't need to build credibility: years and years of experience, or a shopping list of industry contacts. Firstly, if you're new to the industry and you're inquisitive, you leave no stone unturned and you believe everything matters, then your client will see this and you will succeed. Secondly, if you don't have contacts, you simply need to know where to go to make these contacts. You need to be coached. Simple as that. Fundamentally, I believe that it is better to home-grow salespeople from scratch in your business, than to be continually searching for the 'knight on the white horse' type of salesperson — the established superstar salesperson. I say this mainly because those salespeople don't exist, and, if they do, then they're not available to hire. If they're that good, the organisation they're working with today would never let them go. You're better off with a home-grown, well-performing team that has superstars whom you've coached, who understand what being a team player means.

Our Clients Expect Us to Know Their Business

We've touched on this, but now we'll go deeper. The first point is that knowing your client's business is not about having worked with them before. There's a fundamental understanding in business that if you're trying to grow your business, you will have to go and get clients whom you've never worked with before. Clients expect that. As long as you have knowledge of their industry, they will be interested to know if that knowledge is relevant. If you follow this with some knowledge of their business, then you're in the game. But as I stated earlier, we do work in an environment where there are no new customers. So to win a client you need to displace the incumbent. Incumbents are continually being displaced over time, so this is a critical part of sustaining and growing your business. Therefore, the strategy needs to offer something different to the client. Trying to pick a commodity aspect of a deal and doing it faster or cheaper is only a race to the bottom. The strategy that delivers long-term value is:

We are different. We understand.

Some incumbent vendors will fall into the trap of being good at their job, but not being good at understanding their client's business. There are many, many opportunities out there to win clients if you take a short-, medium- and long-term view of that client. You can't just accept that Client X has outsourced work to competitor Y on a contract that has three years left to run and expect to compete for it in three years' time. It's very hard after three years of little or no contact with the client to build credibility, knowledge and trust. It's very rare that a client will trust an organisation that hasn't delivered anything to them before with a $20+ million deal.

The better approach is: 'What can I sell them this week?' That might be a very small $50K piece of work, but you've got to sell them something to build trust, to have a deliverable. It's only when you've demonstrated knowledge and gained trust through delivery that you have the credibility required for those bigger deals. This is a long-term approach, but gone are the days of waiting three years for the big sale alone.

It is also important to develop contacts with your client organisation that are broad and start high. To do a multimillion-dollar deal you need to start at the highest point of responsibility in the organisation, whether it be the COO or the CMO or the CSO, depending on whose initiative it is. You need to start there and then move broadly across the organisation at that level to ensure you have coverage. Any deal of a significant size relative to the organisation's turnover will need to get signed off by a CEO or the board, or both. That's a fundamental truth. The board or the CEO aren't going to sign off on something that their COO and/or CMO and/or CSO hasn't recommended to them. You need to start high in this case, so you can demonstrate your knowledge of the industry, and build that trust to gain credibility. You will also be having better quality conversations in order to best illustrate that you are different and that you do understand.

Alternatively, if you start down low in your client's organisation, then invariably you're not having a quality conversation, you're simply talking technology. You'll be dealing with the IT manager, or the security project officer, whom you have to deal with as well, but it's very hard — near impossible — to improve the quality of this technology conversation and push it up the chain to the CSO, the CEO and the board. You might develop some great contacts here, have some pleasant lunches, and spend a lot of time entertaining, but ultimately it is unlikely these contacts will influence the deal.

Whilst it's not important to have worked with that client before to demonstrate that you have knowledge and understand their business, it is important how you share that knowledge, as there can be inappropriate ways of doing this. You've got to be a storyteller, and you've got to have enough emotional intelligence to understand what to share, when and with whom.

For example, I had a new salesperson whom I took to a client meeting. This was the first time my salesperson was meeting with the head of a client department. I was already credible with this organisation because I had sold them a multimillion-dollar deal. I was there to introduce this new salesperson because he was taking this client over from me. The very first thing the salesperson said to the head of the department was: 'I know all about government purchasing requirements. If you need any help with these, why not give me a call?'

Immediately my hackles went up. This was a statement that doesn't prove knowledge to enable trust and build credibility. What the salesperson was really saying was he knew more about government purchasing requirements than the client head of department. He was lecturing the client, and not working with the client over time to develop credibility. And no one likes to be told they know less about something by the person telling them.

This immediately put the client head of department on the back foot. If my salesperson had said something like: 'Perhaps I'll come back and see you in a month's time and we can talk to you about your experience in government, so I can better understand how your processes work.' That would have given them the opportunity to show knowledge to build trust to gain credibility.

There can also be privacy concerns when you hold knowledge of your client's business. There's no hard and fast rule here. You've got to understand if the knowledge is in the public domain or not, and whether this means you can share it or not. There's always information you pick up on a client just by talking with them. Sometimes you might hear something and think, 'Should I really know this?'

It's human nature for people to want to share their knowledge with you, there may just be times where repeating this knowledge isn't appropriate. My rule of thumb here is that if you are an avid and inquisitive newspaper reader or listener, you are going to learn a massive amount of publicly available information about your client organisation that you can share. So, if in doubt, start and end there in conversation.

You've also got to be mindful at which level you're sharing information. For example, if I talk to someone four levels down from the CEO and I tell them the CEO talked to me about cost efficiencies, they could hear redundancies and sackings for them and their team.

Ultimately, I don't think there's a process to teach how information should be shared appropriately. If someone on your team can't understand what fundamental information is good to share and what isn't, then they might be the wrong person to have on your team. I always say you should hire for emotional intelligence and you can train everything else. This all comes back to credibility. If you're not sharing information appropriately or you're breaching privacy and confidentialities, then you'll lose all your credibility and be out the door, i.e. don't be a gossip.

Being an ex-police officer, I don't believe there's any better method to increase your knowledge of your client's business than through investigation. So get on to the internet, read publications, and get out there and talk to people in the industry. Nothing beats that. If you do these things continually, you'll build up your knowledge pretty quickly because nothing soaks in better than continuous light rain.

You might try to hire the knowledge into your team, which sometimes you have to do, but often this just hits the surface, it doesn't have the same impact. If you've got everyone following this learning process, this continuous light rain will soak through your organisation, and culturally your organisation will learn more about your client's organisation.

One thing *not* to do here is to talk to everyone you can in your client's organisation. Nothing will turn off a client more than if you're in there having general conversations and asking questions that as a student of the industry, who has done the research on the client's business, you should already know the answer to. There are plenty of other salespeople in there doing that.

It's okay to test your knowledge with the client, for example, by asking them if such-and-such is true. This is an important distinction, test what you've learnt rather than ask what you should know. This is important. It comes back to the equation that if you display knowledge to the client, then you will build trust, which will give you credibility and you will stand out from the competition.

Our Clients Expect Us to Invest in Their Success

When we are selling a client an outcome, as opposed to a piece of technology, we need to accept a reasonable degree of responsibility for ensuring our client gets what they need, or gets to where they need to go. There has to be a clear understanding between us, the vendor and our client, as to what success looks like. Contractually, there's going to be a commercial construct, there's going to be a statement of work, and there's going to be a payment structure. These three things are a given and are going to be created during a negotiation process. The one important thing that is often overlooked in this process is:

What does success look like to the client?

I like to use the analogy that you've just bought a new block of land and your dream house is being built on it, and, at the end of the day, success for you is sitting on the balcony, looking over the view, with a glass of wine in your hand. That's success. But neither the commercial constructs, the scope of work, nor the payment structure describe this. So you can have all of these things delivered perfectly. You can own that block of land. You can have your dream house finished. You can have paid it all off. Nothing about these things separately or combined feel like success. None of them describes you at the end of the day sitting on your balcony, looking over the view, with a glass of wine in your hand.

So we need to understand and describe fully what success looks like for our client. I've found the best way to do this is through a series of success workshops. These workshops must involve everyone in your organisation, from the legal people, to the finance people, to the people leader. The entire organisation must understand what success looks like to your client to be able to deliver that success.

The following scenario is an example of why it's important to involve everyone in the organisation. In this case, I'll be the talent acquisition manager. My organisation has just won a deal and I'm tasked with acquiring the talent for that deal. I'm tasked, or told something like: 'You've got 30 days to deliver a project manager or a Microsoft expert that has these skill levels.'

Now I can successfully deliver that project manager with that skill level, but there's no measure that they must fit into my client's organisation. There's no measure that they need to contribute to the vision of success for my client. The project manager I hire could be a complete mismatch for my client, yet I've successfully accomplished my task.

You might think it's unreasonable to expect your entire organisation to understand what success looks like for your client. I know a number of people managers and CFOs that would find this concept confronting. But let me put it this way: there aren't many businesses that don't have two signs hanging on their walls when you first walk in the front door saying something like:

1. Our staff are our most important asset

and

2. Our clients are at the centre of everything we do.

Yet fundamentally the client isn't at the centre of everything they do, because not everyone in the organisation understands what success is for the client. And the staff aren't their most important asset because by not understanding what success looks like for the client, they are delivering projects poorly and are under a bucket-load of stress because they are the ones soaking up the pain of their clients for their organisation. In this scenario the project becomes the most important asset, not the staff.

The truly unfortunate part about all this is our clients understand these untruths. They have become numb to hearing things like: 'We're a client-centric organisation' or 'Our clients are at the centre of everything we do' or 'We have the highest Net Promoter Score in the industry.' Clients hear this as: 'Blah, blah, blah, blah ...' because they're just words. If you implement success workshops across your entire organisation in order to understand what success looks like for your client, then the client will understand you mean what you say, and you will stand out from your competition and you will win more business.

What exactly is a success workshop? A success workshop is a coached session run by an independent person put on in an environment conducive to bringing out the uniqueness of why the work is being done and what will be perceived as success. This workshop will establish clearly defined success metrics for the client.

I know a lot of people who say that a good contract is one that stays in the bottom drawer. I don't believe that. Fundamentally, I think at all times you must deliver on the terms of the contract, but this delivery can be improved by overlaying it with success metrics. These metrics would never take precedence over a contract, but they support it by enabling you to change things when the client environment changes. If you have a multi-year project, then the contract that you negotiated in good faith at the beginning of the first year is probably not fit for purpose at the start of year two or three. If you have an overlay of success metrics which are currently and constantly reviewed, you can see when and where you need to change the contract.

An example of a situation to illustrate this: 75% of the projects I've been involved in measure success, at the end of the day, against organisational change management; yet the contracts for the majority of these projects ignore organisational change management. Only the biggest projects have a requirement for organisational change management built into the contract.

In my view, success metrics should sit around cultural impact in all projects. I've seen projects where the deliverables have successfully been delivered, but the project ultimately failed because the organisational change management wasn't handled well enough. Success metrics are collaborative and need to be developed and continually monitored over time. These are separate from SLAs (Service-Level Agreements) and do not feature deliverables that are time or solution based. They should simply address questions like: How readily was the new deliverable picked up and used by X?

A sentiment index can be implemented through a weekly poll of users, asking them how they're going with the program. This poll can be quick and informal, but I guarantee it will absolutely reflect how well the program's going in their environment, and you will pick up on any problems before they become contractual issues for your client.

I've spent some time talking about delivery because, without a doubt, our clients' expectations are highest at this point. We've made all these promises to illustrate how wonderful the world's going to be for them and they expect us to deliver.

Prior to winning the deal, I don't think there's as clear a method of illustrating our investment in our clients' success other than a clear demonstration that we understand what this success looks like. Alongside demonstrating that we understand the pressures our clients are under in their particular environments. If we can do this well, then we will become someone our clients see as critical and they will turn to us when they need more knowledge about how our solutions and services can enhance their position in the marketplace.

Let me put this another way. There are essentially two things that we worry about in business: our reputation and the experience we're delivering to our clients. So whether you are a retailer or a bank or a mining organisation or a transport organisation, if you have a strong reputation you'll attract clients.

Once you've attracted a client you must deliver a great client experience or the reputation you've created completely falls flat. We've all been to restaurants where the hype was wonderful and we turn up and it is rubbish. The reputation dragged us in, the client experience keeps us there. So, as a selling organisation, we have to understand these two things. Reputation is built with knowledge of the industry, of the ecosystems I've talked about earlier, and knowledge of our client's business. Reputation is maintained through the delivery of a positive client experience that understands what success looks like for the client.

Now I'm not here to tell you that if you do everything right, that if you have a good reputation and success metrics in place for excellent client delivery, then you are going to win every deal. It doesn't work that way. It's a fundamental rule of life that some of our accounts and deals will go nowhere. I estimate this happens in roughly 60% of cases. This will be due to the client not having a budget, or the pain not being great enough for the client to end up doing the deal, or the client will simply go elsewhere. We all lose deals.

There will always be a portion of our effort spent investing in a client's success that won't, today, deliver anything. I say 'today', because it could in the future. I have seen many times where a client has come back to do a deal a year or two after we lost a deal with them. There's no risk in overinvesting in a client when you follow the principles of credibility. Throwing cash at clients for marketing events and taking them overseas, all these things are nearly always a waste of money if you don't have an absolutely robust plan of: knowledge + trust = credibility.

For example, some time ago there was a large law firm in Melbourne who wanted to move their environment into the cloud. There's a lot of legislation around this concerning privacy. We were able to meet those legislative concerns. We invested in this deal over a long period of time, but in the end we didn't win. We weren't able to meet their requirements well enough for them to trust us doing this piece of work. Probably our sales process could have been enhanced, but anyway, you don't win every deal.

We did, however, build a lot of credibility with the client. A year later, they needed a new CRM and they came exclusively to us. At some point in the cloud deal, we were able to demonstrate that we really understood the issues around reputation and client experience. We must have been able to demonstrate this better than we were able to demonstrate our methodology for moving them into the cloud. We missed one selling opportunity but overall we created another.

A key to achieving this was that we continued to engage with the client. We didn't lose the deal and walk away. I always encourage my sales teams to continue to engage with clients where they've lost deals because it can deliver success in the long term. It really comes back to being a student of the industry. It has to be at the appropriate level and at the appropriate rate. It's not about being a nuisance. Clients are generally more prepared to share things with you when they know you're investing in them more than you're investing in the opportunities they create.

A caveat: not all clients will want to buy what you're selling. If you're getting a really clear message early on that your client doesn't want you to invest in their success, then walk away. There's a lot of business out there and it's a matter of picking the right clients to sell to, that have similar cultures and imperatives to yours. Walking *away* from deals is just as important as walking *to* deals, but we sometimes do this too late.

So how do we ensure that we're working on the right deals? How do we justify the ROI (Return On Investment) for the time spent? For example, say the first deal you win from a client is a $50K consulting deal, and to win this deal you might have invested, in time and effort, say up to a couple of hundred thousand dollars. This is a devastatingly low ROI looking at the dollar figures alone. But look at it this way: you invested up to a couple of hundred thousand dollars, not for this one $50K deal, but to learn and to get involved with this client.

It's also created some momentum. That first deal has shown you've got knowledge, the delivery has inspired trust, and this is transferable within that client's organisation. It's also transferable within the industry because people move around. So while the investment is outweighed by the return in the early days, it's setting you up for further opportunities and they will come. The premise here is that there's no short-term fix. It could be a number of years before this momentum really picks up and you land a $20+ million deal. ROI has to be viewed over a long period of time.

For example, I was working in Canberra where I knew a government networking tender was coming up for renewal in three years' time. A large Australian telco was the incumbent. We invested in getting to know the client environment by hiring some staff who knew that environment. We also brought in a number of local and overseas experts who knew multi-faceted, multi-security level networks. We started having conversations with the client around our experience — the storytelling. We sold them little pieces of work, here and there. All this built-up momentum for us. It took three years and we won that tender hands down. We invested heavily up front and it paid off. It was a $20 million a year contract that grew to $35 million once the associated services were added. If we had made an ROI decision at the one- or two- or even near three-year stage, we would have pulled the plug then and there and missed out on the deal.

A lot of organisations have deal review boards or similar, where salespeople bring in deals to be reviewed. I think these mechanisms are long out of date and regularly deliver the wrong outcome. If you follow a process where you have a strategy that is well defined for each client alongside the opportunities you are going to pursue with these clients, then the opportunities will qualify themselves in or out of their own accord. As long as you have enough people in your organisation who are allocated to that client's success, then there will be a continual and ongoing review process that will develop beyond a black-and-white start point to become iterative over time.

Our Clients Expect a Modular Solution

If you're selling $20+ million services deals, then you've seen an evolution in the marketplace. Probably only five years ago, organisations would come to market to outsource their entire environment. For example, their desktop environment. Today they are coming to market having broken their entire environment down into three or four areas. Each of these areas is referred to as a module. The client will create a different tender for each module, and they can decide to select a different vendor for each.

The effect of a move to modular solutions is that contract sizes are getting smaller. There is still the same amount of money out there, but there's more competition for it. This has happened because clients have realised from experience that there's no single vendor that can deliver on the promise across the entire environment.

It's still possible for one vendor to win all of the parts of the environment, but it's unlikely because the competition from the smaller to mid-sized vendors is fierce. Five years ago, these smaller to mid-sized players didn't have the skills across the entire environment to compete for the entire environment, and neither did they have deep enough pockets for the insurance and liability. All this has changed.

So there are many, many vendors that are now capable of competing on deals. Some of these vendors focus on the technology and the cost. In the IT industry we call these vendors 'box droppers'. There are many examples of these vendors running environments today that are modularised and delivering great outcomes for clients. Yet because the deal was won in a commodity sense, as opposed to winning it in a value sense, these box droppers have given up predict-ability for their business pipeline.

For example, you could be talking to a purchasing officer, and they say, 'I can buy an iPhone from XYZ for $2 cheaper than your iPhones and I want to buy 1,000 of them. Can you meet that price?' There are only two answers you can give them. But if you're having a conver-sation around delivering an *outcome*, then you're taking price or commodity out of the conversation. You're also likely to be having this conversation at a senior level. This not only makes you valuable to the client, but it also means you're likely to find out about other opportunities in the business before the box droppers, and early iden-tification is crucial to landing the big deals. It will also help with your annual revenue. It will make your business pipeline more predict-able because you will have a better understanding of the upcoming opportunities.

So what's the next evolution in the marketplace beyond modular solutions? I can see a time in the not-so-distant future when client contracts are going to have the equivalent of AI (Artificial Intelli-gence) or machine-learning built into them. These AI contracts will evolve as the business conditions change and we all know business conditions are always changing.

This will require a mature approach from both the client and the vendor and will be based on client success. Client success will need to be established as a metric through regularly held and regularly monitored success workshops. These ongoing success workshops will quickly determine whether what we think of as success today will carry forward into the future. If this success doesn't carry forward, then the AI contract will immediately change, changing the processes in place to ensure and protect future success.

Obviously, this approach will require significant investment on both sides and I don't underestimate the sophistication and level of willingness from both parties to engage with this. It will not be an easy transition for the industry and is definitely something I consider is well into the future, but once, and if, it's established, it will pay back this investment by providing longevity in the contract. It will also ensure the contract, and indeed the mutual dependence, will evolve into something that is well beyond what any competitor can dislodge. Importantly, it will give back that downtime when contracts are being manually renegotiated. I've seen a lot of missed opportunities on both sides during this time.

Our Clients Expect a Personalised Solution

Our clients are looking to be more flexible in the way they procure most things. The modular approach allows them to do this. When our clients buy modular solutions from a number of different vendors, rather than from one, they are not constricted by a major head contract. This, in turn, increases the amount of ownership each vendor has on each outcome, and each vendor is able to behave in a more client orientated and personalised manner, which increases the flexibility for the client.

This style of engagement is still maturing in the marketplace and one implication is that our clients — to essentially avoid their multiple vendors' fingers pointing at each other when there are unsatisfactory outcomes — must put a lot more work into understanding what the outcomes need to be for each module and how those outcomes work together. The evolution to success metrics, as opposed to SLAs, into the future will enable clients to better manage these multiple outcomes.

Our clients also understand that to get economies of scale, they still have to take some level of a generic solution. This generic part of the solution is the foundational part and it sits underneath the personalised part, as summarised in the following diagram.

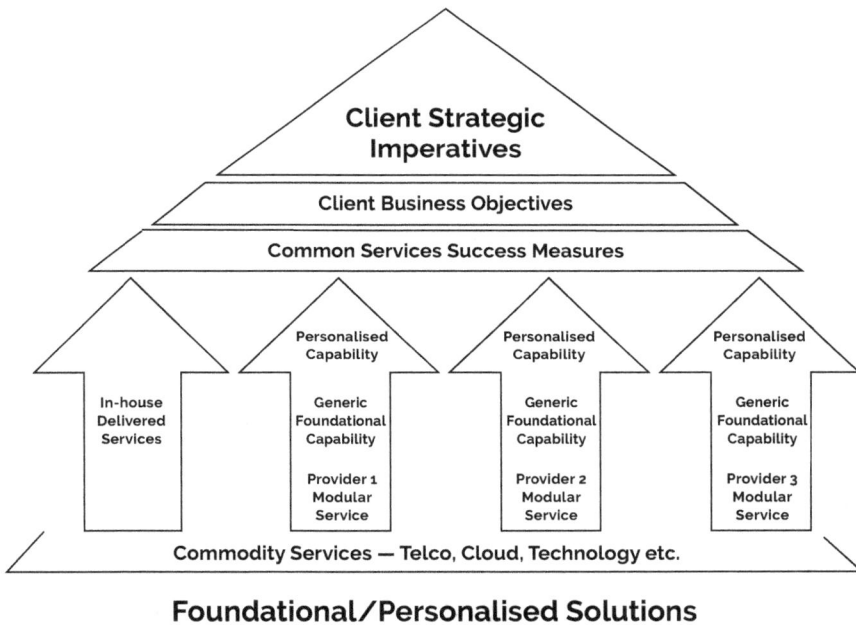

Foundational/Personalised Solutions

As mentioned previously, we know that our clients don't get up in the morning and decide they want to go and build an XYZ or develop something. This isn't what they've come to market for, this is the foundational part of the solution. Our clients wake in the morning wanting to achieve an outcome that's going to form part of meeting their strategic imperatives into the future. This is what they've really come to market for, this is the personalised part of the solution.

Let me put this another way: how do I deliver a robust enterprise-class solution? That's the foundational part. How do I ensure this enterprise-class solution is tailored well enough to meet the long-term strategic direction of the client? That's the personalised part.

Personalisation has completely changed the way vendors manage large-scale contracts. In the past I've seen many examples where it was cheaper for a vendor to miss an SLA and pay the penalty, than it was for them to meet that agreement to achieve the client outcome. The vendor never did enough to get kicked out, but they didn't do enough to achieve the client outcome. This led to an adversarial relationship.

The personalised solution changes this dynamic. It enables the client to be flexible enough to meet their changing commercial needs without the significant impost of a major contractual change. For example, if the client is a bank and they suddenly need to acquire an insurance company to improve their market footprint, or they're going to acquire a smaller bank in a different state or region to improve their overall commercial viability (pending regulatory approval), the personalised solution enables them to do this without wearing a number of penalties for changing the scope of the contract.

Ultimately, with a personalised solution our clients are expecting us, their vendors, to take on the responsibility and the risk to actually deliver the outcome. The box-dropping days, where you don't take on the risk of delivering the outcome, you simply drop the box, are numbered in terms of maintaining a sustainable margin. Box droppers will continue into the future but will become increasingly marginalised and commoditised.

To deliver outcomes, vendors need to embrace risk and ensure they have the right level of resources and team members to deliver what they said they were going to deliver, as part of that personalised solution for the client. The upside of embracing this risk and delivering the outcome are the flow-on benefits I described earlier. The vendor's reputation will be enhanced. The vendor will create a more positive environment for the people who work in their organisation. Tenure and culture and all those things at that organisation will be significantly enhanced. And, importantly, they will then be in a much better position to go out and win new business.

I think it's the smaller providers in the marketplace today that are best placed to deliver personalised solutions for their clients. I don't believe that all the global multinationals have the ability to be flexible enough to be able to meet this new paradigm. I also think the smaller providers will use better resources. What I have seen from the global multinationals is that, generally speaking, from a delivery point of view, it's the lowest common denominator. How cheap can I get the resources I need to deliver, so I can achieve the best margin?

Every deal I have lost, I have lost because I only answered the documentation, the foundational part, but I didn't answer the personalised part. I wasn't able to contextualise that to the client because I didn't have the knowledge. The client comes to market with a series of requirements in the documentation that they are ready and keen to talk about. These requirements are obviously important and you must talk about them well, but the client rarely talks further about the wider, personal outcome they want to achieve for their organisation. That's our job to find that out. You must engage long-term with the client and have those deeper conversations. If you don't, then you're just receiving the documentation and you can only respond to that, which is what everybody else is doing. This is the opposite of a personalised solution. It becomes a commoditised race to the bottom on price.

2. Our Competitors

Competition has always been hard and intense. This hasn't changed but the nature of this competition has. Which I believe is a good thing because it should therefore deliver better outcomes for the client. Ten years or so ago, competition would be between two or three major multinationals and maybe one or two Australian tier-two players, whereas now there are many more players and often these players are small and nimble.

The result is, as vendors, we've still got to be on our game price-wise, solution-wise, and within the commercials, which has always been the case, but — given that deals are being broken down — we're also now having to compete for more of these smaller deals, rather than just the one big mega deal. This is driving the cost of responding up, because effectively it's just as much effort and requires similar resources to compete on a smaller deal than the mega deal, and with the same level of staffing we must therefore focus more on our approaches.

We need to improve the ways we are qualifying out of the deals that don't match our capabilities. We should also be partnering with organisations that can help us improve our capabilities where we need to. As a result, there's a much greater level of 'coopetition' (cooperative competition) today. We partner with someone today and compete against them tomorrow. This is a very sound approach to doing business because it provides a better outcome for the client.

Larger Deals Being Broken Down into Smaller Deals

I feel I need to go into more detail here, as it's not only modular solutions that are driving the breakdown of larger deals into smaller deals. In his maiden speech to the Australian Information Industry Association delivered at the National Press Club in Canberra on 13 June 2018, Michael Keenan, Head of the Digital Transformation Agency, which is the government's IT authority, ruled that government deal sizes were not to exceed $100 million in total contract value over three years.[1] There could be extensions on this, but that was the maximum size.

Whereas previously, organisations like the Department of Defence, or the ATO, or the Department of Human Services would regularly come to market with $100+ million deals. There are some exceptions to this, but, as a general rule, deal sizes over time have been broken down significantly by this ruling. The three-year contracting term is also a change. In the past, contracts could be over a five-year period with a plus two, plus another two, plus another one, so over ten years.

Inevitably, this gave the vendor a lot of leeway to hold back initial investment and get away with doing so for two to three years. The vendor would then spend for a year to improve things, then hold back for a year, then spend up big for the last year of the five to get the extension. With three-year contracts the vendor must get up and running in the first six to eight months, or they are going to be shown the door straight away.

---

1   https://ministers.pmc.gov.au/keenan/2018/
     delivering-australias-digital-future

Many industry changes start off within government, then move out to enterprise as time goes on, which is happening with the size of deals as well. Bigger deals are being broken down into smaller deals across the board. This, of course, doesn't mean there's less overall money out there as the IT spend of most organisations is going up. It simply means there are a larger number of deals. I've touched on this, but this change means you've got to improve the method of determining which deals you qualify for.

There are a lot of 'guaranteed methods' out there to help us, and most of them talk about 'qualifying deals in'. I'll go into a lot more detail about this later in this book, but I think that we need to change the pendulum here. I think we need to include every deal and then qualify them out. We will naturally be more rigorous and targeted when taking things out of the basket, as opposed to putting things into the basket. It's a psychological shift. We all like to fill baskets rather than empty them, and this change will sharpen our critical judgment to ensure we are left with only the deals we must have.

The other shift that helps us qualify deals is to move the sales target onto the client, which I will examine in more detail later in this book. By doing this, we build up a team of Client Experts who have credibility with the client and are in the perfect position to qualify the wrong deals out. In the current competitive environment qualifying out the wrong deals is critical. Especially when you consider the higher cost of responding, that our clients are expecting personalised solutions, and that roughly 60% of the opportunities out there go nowhere because the client decides to do nothing.

A real positive of deals being broken down into smaller deals is this often gives you better penetration into the client's organisation. In the past a large deal often spread you thinly and widely across the organisation, whereas winning a smaller deal usually implies it's in your expert area, and you can go much deeper into that area with the client. This builds credibility with the client that allows you to move into other areas. You can grow out from there with a lower competitive effort.

In the old days you either won or lost a deal, but today you can win and draw in some cases. For example, in the old days there was one mega deal. Today it might be broken down into four smaller deals. In the old days you either landed the mega deal or you did not, you either won or lost. Today you might pick up only one of those four smaller deals. I consider this a draw, as you're now in with the client and you've got the opportunity to continue to sell to the client. And if you're truly focused on the client's outcomes, and you've got a contract that will evolve to meet the client's changing needs and your competitors do not, then you've got the opportunity to influence the client and bring more business your way. So you might turn one of the deals you lost into a draw and possibly a win.

For example, I had a client who wanted eight towers built, so they broke the deal into eight and went to market for three. These first three were the fundamental building towers and the five following were supply towers. We won all three of them. By bidding on one tower first, we were able to absolutely draw right down to the basement, as it were, the components of the deal. We were able to have specific compartmentalised conversations. Whereas, had it been one large deal across eight towers, it would have been a much more generic conversation that would have ended up being more about the numbers than the outcome.

The Rise of the Niche Player

I have a recent example. There is what I'd describe as a great innovative start-up based in the US that specialises in law enforcement software founded by a couple of friends. They started the business in their teens and it's been going for ten years. They started off with one solution, then they built out to cover all the law-enforcement solutions. At the time of writing they had won a number of police force software tenders across the US. They're a small company with a few big financial backers, but they're still in their seed-funding stage.

An Australian police force recently came to market to acquire a modernised and complete operations system to replace their current one. At the time a large global IT systems integrator was the prime contractor, but they didn't have the expertise to deliver the entire system, so they created a relationship with the innovative US start-up.

This is the perfect arrangement. The Global IT systems integrator has pockets deep enough to pursue the deal and take the risk, whilst the small start-up has the expertise. This is the classic example of a niche player, a small start-up, rising up to compete and win against the bigger players. Collectively, they added value to each other that wasn't able to be surpassed by the other competitors. Ten years ago there were some examples of this, but nothing as dramatic.

The digital world has levelled the playing field for the niche player. It gives greater access to people and expertise, allows a greater level of deal prospecting, and also allows information to be disbursed further. It also enables all vendors to have the same level of marketing presence. Cloud platforms have also enabled this as they give everyone the same level of capability. It also gives the client the ability to put their toe in the water, or try a solution, without having to invest hundreds of millions of dollars to build the infrastructure to trial an application upon it. Now the client can just spin up some machines, trial the application, check its latency over a number of sites, see how it runs and then either rip it down or continue to build. These things are aids and, whether you're a niche player or whether you're an established player, these aids are nothing in themselves if they don't continue to address the client need and sell the overall outcome.

Ultimately the rise of the niche player is fuelling this increase in the number of competitors for every deal today. It is also driving up the intensity of this competition because the niche player has the bandwidth to spend more time to tailor their solution. So not only are there more players for deals today than ten years ago, all players are competing harder to win the deals.

Commoditised Delivery

In IT there's always going to be a commodity layer because the same people can be hired by different vendors to deliver the same outcome to the client. There's essentially a finite pool of delivery talent in the industry, who move across organisations. Therefore, the only way to differentiate your offer is to turn this delivery into a client capability that fits with the client's strategic imperatives. The vendor that is less about delivering hardware or proprietary applications, and more about developing systems, processes and outcomes that ensure their entire team better understands their clients and their strategic imperatives, is more likely to succeed today.

I'll use the analogy of building your dream house again. When you hire the builder, you just assume the builder, or their people, knows how to lay bricks, and that they have access to buy bricks and mortar, and the mortar will dry and it will be perfect. This is more than commoditised delivery, it's assumed delivery.

I've sold to clients who are still contracting on the bricks and the mortar and who lays them. But the modern clients who come to market are contracting on what their business outcomes are. They are asking, 'I want to build a house with a decent view.' And I say, 'Oh, have you considered how many storeys you'd like the house to be? I think it should be at least two because, at the end of the day, when you're out on the balcony with a glass of wine in your hand, you'll enjoy that view so much more.'

PART B:
THE ORGANISATION

3. Our Sales Team

When I first joined the IT industry over 20 years ago, we had account plans, individual quotas, overlay quotas, gates, closed compensation plans, special incentives and so on. And whilst all of these things might look slightly different in different organisations, today they are all essentially in place. Little about the sales approach has changed in the last 20 years. When we consider how far our clients' expectations have shifted during this time, yet this sales approach has not, this alone should be ringing alarm bells.

Are our clients, as a whole, happy? I meet very few who are. Yet the industry carries on in the same way, probably because of reports like the one published on the website *Medium*, based on Bain & Company research,[2] where 80% of CEOs believe they deliver a superior customer experience. Which is great for a CEO to hear, but according to the same research only 8% of their clients agree — 8% underlined.

When we view this alongside my experience that roughly 30% of all IT salespeople don't sell anything each year, 50% sell something but don't get their quota, and it's only the remaining 20% who sell enough to get their quota, then it's a broken system. Anywhere else this would be totally unacceptable. To use an everyday example: if your car only started 30% of the time you tried to start it, what would you do?

In this next section I'm going to outline the key indicators of a sales team that hasn't adapted to meet the challenges of the sales

---

2   https://medium.com/@CMcVoy/80-of-ceos-believe-they-deliver-superior-customer-experience-661efabd16b0

environment today. Some organisations will have a number of these indicators, others might have them all, whilst others might have only one. And whilst organisations will continue in the short term to survive and even be successful carrying these indicators, they will reach a time in the future when eliminating all of them will become business critical.

I'm not advocating an overnight change, these changes are cultural and will take time, but the bottom line in the current market environment is that not one of these indicators can be carried long term. I say this primarily because the competition has intensified with the rise of the nimble and focused niche players and only 8% of clients believing they receive a 'superior customer experience'. The first key indicator is:

A Short-Term View

Twelve months is a short-term view and this view is prevalent across the entire industry. This view is created when we give 12-month targets to every salesperson. Now there's a science involved to this around what their clients bought last year and how those deals were broken up and what the future potential looks like. This potential is then modified by an uplift factor to create the target that's then given out to each member of the sales team.

The majority of salespeople will then develop a straight account plan that only addresses getting that level of revenue in the 12-month period, or the level of margin, depending on how their target is set up. And these targets reset every 12 months. It's like you turn the lights out on June 30, then turn them back on again on July 1 — or

3. Our Sales Team

December 31, then January 1, depending on whether the sales targets are set across the fiscal or calendar year. There's nothing in these 12-month targets that looks at client outcomes. In an environment that is changing, where we need to ensure that we are coupling our success to the client's success, this short-term view is not conducive to the long-term success for our clients.

Let me share how this approach works in practice. Within this 12-month target, commissions are paid monthly. If I'm a salesperson and I haven't sold anything in a month, I'm probably feeling okay. If I don't sell anything in six months, then I start to feel the pressure, I start to feel uncomfortable because nothing structurally changes in my organisation to help me achieve the number. The pressure simply goes up, and after maybe nine months of not selling anything I might get a performance plan.

Now I'm doing my best to perform, I know my manager wants better performance, but there's nothing in that plan to help effect a change. Effectively, there's no other mechanism than the fiscal number to measure my performance, which is very black and white. I either get the number, or I don't. So at the nine-month stage without a sale I'm becoming increasingly desperate to do so. I'm in with my client trying to sell anything I can. I'm not having strategic and long-term conversations. There's no long-term plan that has milestones along the way that includes deals I'm going to win to continually deliver revenue or gross profit. I only want a sale, any sale.

I'm also working hard with my manager to ensure she understands I have significant deals in my future pipeline. I'm convincing her that she can't get rid of me because I've got all these future deals that I'm going to close. And because I'm desperate, I might finally get a sale by undercutting on price. It's a sale where I know I'm selling what I've got, not what the client necessarily wants, but I've convinced them. I also need to convince my manager on the price. I tell her it's a strategic deal that's going to get me the next deal and we've just got to take the lower margin. I won't make commission on the deal, but I may just keep my job. It all goes through and a little bit of the pressure comes off, as I now have a number, not my target number, but at least I'm not part of the 30% who haven't sold anything.

Further, the culture of the sales team is completely shot. Three-quarters are nervous, unhappy and desperate for any sale. They aren't even close to delivering good client outcomes because this nervousness and desperation leads to bad behaviours. The clients are therefore unhappy because they aren't receiving what they increasingly expect: a long-term commitment to their strategic imperatives. Management above the sales team aren't happy because there's no reliability or predictability to the pipeline because the sales team are essentially fudging it to keep their jobs.

I guarantee that if you ask any CEO today: 'How reliable is the pipeline as you measure it over any eight-week period?' The vast majority would reply: 'I don't rely on the pipeline.' If you asked the same question of the sales managers, the vast majority would answer: 'I don't rely upon anything from my sales team; I just make it up.' This is the system we have in place currently. From my experience, in real terms, up to 90% of the future pipeline simply evaporates each year. This has a hugely detrimental effect on the margin, profit and growth of the entire organisation.

It also means that, as a CEO, you cannot stand up in front of the investors or the board or the market, and say with any certainty that, 'I'm going to deliver that 15% growth to the bottom line in our chosen solution sets that I promised last year.'

Here's a specific example. I was involved in a $4 million federal government deal for services and equipment where, at the end of the process, we were sitting across from the client who told us: 'We need you to drop 10% out of this deal before we can award it to you.' This meant dropping it below the threshold of our commission basis, which essentially meant selling for no benefit to anyone in our organisation. No one would get rewarded for this deal. We were desperate enough to get the cash because it was a large proportion of our quota number, which ensured we all kept our jobs into the following year. So we did the deal.

By giving it away like this, we created within our own organisation a reluctance to deliver all the services that would normally be given to a client. In fact, we had some disparate parts of the organisation trying to claw margin back by delivering a lower level of resourcing. In this case, we bid with five people nominated for the delivery, but we hired only three, and they took twice as long to deliver anyway, so there was no real cost saving, just delays.

Ultimately, the deal was delivered under duress, which created a bad outcome for the client. It was a bad outcome for us as well, all based upon the fact that there was no long-term approach to selling, which meant we were selling purely on price. We were commoditised.

A Hero Mentality

There is still a vision in the IT industry today that there is this hero salesperson floating around in the marketplace, and that if only we had that salesperson on board, we would be successful. So we transfer our entire expectation of making the sales target to a need to hire this hero. I've had managers say to me: 'Andrew, go and hire me the best salesperson in the industry.'

So off I go trying to find the best, and I'm focused on that so I forget about my own targets. Or, if we have that hero salesperson in our organisation, we give them all the time and resources they want. The one thing we don't do is hold them to account to share all of the information to ensure that everything's on track and we're going to get our number. That's not how we handle these hero salespeople. We leave them alone to weave their magic because they're 'wonderful' and 'gifted' — not.

For example, I was involved in an opportunity with a public-sector organisation in Asia that we ultimately lost. In that deal, I was working alongside a local salesperson who had won one or two big deals — reputational deals. He was our lead salesperson on this deal. When I met him, I asked how we were going with it. I questioned and questioned and questioned him, and he kept delaying and delaying. He had the hero mentality and the hero status in the organisation, and because of that he didn't have a great sales plan for the deal. Had we been allowed to open his plan up for really critical review and analysis every step of the way, then we might have won the deal. But that's not how a hero works.

The hero is very inwardly looking and secretive in their approach. They lack documentation and strategic review because their reputation allows them to get away with it. They also often begin to believe that *they* are the difference. Sometimes you can land a big deal and not really know for sure what got you across the line. It could have been any combination of factors. And even though we do win-and-loss reviews, from my experience, we enter these reviews with our beliefs already formed, unless the client is very mature, which is rare. These reviews therefore tend to reinforce our already-held beliefs, rather than uncover the actual reasons for the win or loss. Given the hero status is already within these beliefs, these reviews tend to reinforce the hero status, rather than examine whether it was the hero who actually won, or lost, the deal.

Like everyone who has worked in IT, I've lived this model. On my first day in Canberra IT sales in 1998 there was a mega deal that had just been landed, and the sales lead on it was a guy called Bill. I was a junior salesperson and everyone around me was saying: 'Look at Bill! Look at Bill! Isn't he great?' And he was swanning about having coffee with everyone, you know, working everyone over like a sporting hero.

Perhaps it was my police background, having only been a couple of years out of the force at that stage, but I looked at Bill and thought, 'What's going on here? He's just a show pony.' But, being new to the industry, I thought that must be what you do. That's how to behave. And all because he won this big deal everyone wanted to talk with him. When I asked him about method or process, he deflected. To this day no one knows how he won that big deal. It was the only deal he landed in the time I worked with him, and two years later he was let go.

I've been that hero salesperson. Early on I won a lot of deals on my own and achieved my targets. I was in the Unisys Presidents Club, won a lot of awards and they felt good. Really good. You make lots of money and get everything you need from the organisation and the people around you, whether you know what you're doing or not. It wasn't until I became a manager that I realised a hero mentality simply doesn't work. When I began mentoring my team, I quickly realised that you can't have a team full of heroes. A hero mentality is great for the individual but is toxic for the team. I also realised it is often circumstances that dictate success for the individual salesperson and that, in the long run, strategy and teamwork are the more important components of success.

As a manager, I also realised that the hero salesperson has a lot in common with the failing salesperson. If you ask the hero salesperson to get you a meeting with their number-one client, they will rarely deliver. There will always be an excuse like their client is out of town, or at a conference. The failing salesperson will behave the same way. The hero salesperson doesn't keep thorough documentation or their sales CRM up-to-date. They will make the excuse that it's all in their heads and avoid sharing it with you. The failing salesperson does the same. The hero salesperson can be viewed as a failing salesperson who has been lucky enough to land one or two mega deals. Nothing more.

There is a salesperson in between the hero and the failing, one I'd describe as the pragmatic salesperson. This salesperson predominantly fills that 50% of salespeople who don't reach their target, but do make a sale. This salesperson may not be selling strategically, but they fall back on a robust process. They make 20 phone calls a day, get to four meetings and deliver three proposals a week, and follow up on all of their proposals 10 times the following week. They simply do the work. If a CEO hired a team with only these pragmatic salespeople in it, then the organisation would probably be better off. They may or may not land the mega deals, which sometimes you need to get across the line at the end of the year, but ultimately the predictability would be a better outcome for the organisation than relying on the hero salesperson.

I'd like to take this a step further and suggest there's a fourth category of salesperson that would be far more successful. These are what I term 'Client Experts'. Client Experts are digital natives who understand the value digital presents in terms of cyber, automation and artificial intelligence. They are able to contextualise these trends to their clients at the highest level. They understand that even when they land the mega deal, they aren't heroes because they're working in a process that's replicable, that can be automated and is utterly team based.

This shift towards a team-based approach will enable greater predictability for the organisation because information will be better shared. A team of people will better explain which deals they've won or lost in the past with the client, and be in a better position to predict whether they can land the current deal than an individual salesperson. This will remove a lot of responsibility from the sales individual to deliver the sale, which effectively means less commission for salespeople. This is a big cultural shift, and I'd argue that although there will be less commission for a salesperson per sale, there will be more sales, so salespeople won't be worse off. And we will reduce the 30% of salespeople that don't make a sale. I will be going into a lot more detail around Client Experts and commissions later in this book.

Relationship-Only Selling

I've touched on this earlier and now I'll go deeper. IT organisations are fixated on having relationships. We have Digital Relationship Managers, Client Relationship Managers, Account Relationship Managers, Customer Relationship Managers — you name it. Yet relationships are built on being liked, which, as I've said previously, is a transient and fickle state. In a relationship, things can go sour very quickly even by saying one wrong thing one day.

Relationships can also move. If I'm a salesperson with a relationship in a client organisation with X, and X moves to another organisation, then the entire strategy with that client, which was poor from the beginning, evaporates. Relationships also tend to be singular and contained. If X sees me talking to someone else in X's organisation, then they might become a little jealous, or concerned about what it means for the relationship. And mostly, relationships are built lower down in the organisation, which, given their singularity, means the salesperson can't move upward in the organisation to where they need to engage. We need to remove the word 'relationship' from the corporate vocabulary and replace it with credibility. A salesperson needs to prove their value at the highest level in the client organisation and spread out from there by proving knowledge to gain trust to build credibility.

We can still have lunch with our clients. Social functions are worthwhile. We all form relationships with our clients. I'm not saying we shouldn't be friendly and liked, but credibility must come first. A relationship without credibility is the issue. It is the relationship-only salesperson who relies solely on these social events as a mechanism to sell.

They also function like a dating agent. They are always asking for pre-sale resources. They are looking for the expert to qualify out the deal for them. They might begin with: 'Hi, Chris. Thank you for seeing me. How are the husband and kids? How was your weekend?' Chris replies, 'Oh, I got up to this and I did this and that.' The salesperson adds, 'That's great. I'd now like to introduce you to Andrew. Andrew is our expert on artificial intelligence. Andrew, tell Chris about artificial intelligence.'

Qualifying the deal is 100% the domain of the salesperson. As I've stated before, the salesperson must know the industry and where their client sits in that industry, and understand their own organisation and where their value lies within that organisation. It's only when all these things match up and the client has a requirement or an outcome based upon these things, that a deal can be qualified. You don't need anyone else to do this, unless you don't know enough about the industry or the client. I've rarely seen a relationship-only salesperson qualify a deal themselves. They just don't have the knowledge.

The relationship-only salesperson always says 'yes' to the client, even when the answer should be 'no'. 'Yes, I'll get you some pre-sales. Yes, we'll get a pilot going. Yes, I can discount the deal. Yes. Yes. Yes.' This is because the relationship-only salesperson relies on being liked and saying 'no' could damage the relationship. This can lead to a lot of wasted time and resources that ultimately damages the margin. Whereas the salesperson who has built credibility is able to say something along the lines of: 'Actually I don't think that's the right way to go.' Because they know enough about the industry and enough about the solution to say, 'I think you need to be thinking about this, and I can't give you that, because we would need to do this first.' And through their knowledge they are able to link the things that need to happen first to the client outcomes in a logical and successful way.

Earlier in my IT career, I hired relationship-based salespeople. It used to work. When I was working in Canberra over 10 years ago, I wanted to grow my footprint across the market. I needed a fast way to break into new accounts, so I looked around the marketplace for people who had the right relationships in the accounts that I wanted. Through some contacts, I felt that I found the right person. When I hired him, he became one of the higher paid salespeople in my organisation. I had to get the CEO to sign off on his employment contract.

Over the following months, we won some substantial business. We were able to grow that contract to several multiples of the original win. Throughout this time, my salesperson maintained his relationships, typically in a very protective manner, and notably mostly failed to get the client to corporate events. As the agency evolved, as all clients do, the salesperson's relationships weakened, and so did the pipeline. Eventually, the salesperson left the company.

A few years later, I hired another salesperson whom I knew had previously been a relationship-only salesperson. Through the interview process I thought she had evolved into a credibility-based salesperson; unfortunately, this didn't turn out to be the case. From the day she arrived, she insisted that pre-sales go with her to all meetings. I felt she was playing the dating game. In her head, she seemed to be telling herself: 'Hello, smart client, meet smart specialist, and I will sit back and think about what I'll have when I take you to lunch.'

This didn't deliver any value for the clients and, after some time passed, nothing had been sold. My credibility with the CEO took a hit with this, as I'd hired this person, and ultimately it reinforced to me that relationship-only selling doesn't work anymore.

As clients transition from buying equipment to buying solutions and outcomes that fit with their strategic imperatives, it really is the end of the road for the relationship-only salesperson. Clients no longer buy from people they like; they buy from people who understand and can articulate the outcome they require. This is a complex paradigm that requires deep knowledge from the salesperson to enable them to build trust at the upper levels of the client organisation. Whilst there will always be people at client organisations up for an expensive lunch, this alone no longer guarantees a sale today.

A Solely Opportunistic Mentality

A salesperson with a solely opportunistic mentality wakes up each day and asks themselves: 'What is my client buying today?' They aren't interested in anything other than that. There's a bit of a joke in the industry that refers to these salespeople as 'Those that wait by the fax machine.' They don't have a strategy nor a plan for their client, they are simply lucky enough that they have a client who continues to buy what they're selling.

These salespeople can be wildly successful. They can gain great status in their organisation, making their number each year and earning great commissions. But ultimately these salespeople are simply order takers. They are responding solely to what the client thinks they need. They don't challenge the client. They don't have conversations about their client's long-term strategic imperatives. They are very busy and very active and are very good at being immersed in the client, but they aren't delivering anything back to the client other than product.

Now, as a CEO, you might say, 'Well, if we had a whole crew of these salespeople, it would be perfect. We'll make our number each year and everything will be great.' The problem with this approach is, given the relationship is one sided, that it relies solely on the client buying. It becomes unpredictable because once the client stops buying, which often happens, there's no lever to bring them back. It's also a vulnerable relationship because — given the opportunistic salesperson is simply an order taker who doesn't add value beyond attentiveness — there's very little client loyalty. In this situation a competitor can easily come in and steal that client by undercutting on price.

I've used 'solely' pointedly in this section's heading because all salespeople are, to some degree, opportunistic and need to be; it's part of doing business. For example, if I'm working with a client longterm on the two things they want most, which we talked about earlier — firstly, to enhance their reputation in the marketplace; secondly, to deliver an exceptional client experience — then we're having these conversations and along the way they ask: 'Hey, we've got to buy XYZ. Do you sell these?' And, of course, we do sell XYZ, so I make the sale. I might not have seen that sale coming, so it's an opportunistic sale. Admittedly, it grew out of the fact that I'm credible with the client, and have developed trust and knowledge, and have positioned myself as part of the client's future, so it was natural that it flowed to me.

This is what I call the 'cream'. The opportunistic salesperson deals solely with this cream. That's all they want and know. I guarantee that if a solely opportunistic salesperson from a competitor tried to come in and win that same XYZ sale, they would have failed. In this case, they didn't see it coming. But even if they had, and even if they tried to undercut me on price, I guarantee the client would still have given me the option on the sale within their procurement guidelines. It was a natural outcome given the conversations we were having. So the distinction here is about behaviour. The salespeople I'm talking about here display only opportunistic behaviour, whereas other salespeople might display opportunistic behaviour on occasion, but they display a range of other behaviours as well.

The other important point here is that we should never undervalue the area of the market that the solely opportunistic salesperson operates in. It's very important to cover the entire gambit of the marketplace. Winning the commodity deals when the client is buying is very important and the solely opportunistic salesperson can be very skilful winning these deals. Hence their success in the marketplace today. It's important not only to win these deals because they bring in significant revenue, but they also keep your competitors away from the client. It allows you alone to establish a presence with the client to learn their long-term strategic imperatives and build credibility to secure the long-term deals. This is especially important given there's no new clients.

A commodity deal is the perfect entry point to steal a client away from a competitor to grow your business. And, as I've said earlier, winning these deals solely, which a solely opportunistic salesperson can do, might keep their organisation in business in the short to medium term, but over time there will be increased downward pressure on margins and therefore profit.

Remember that 92% of our clients aren't fully satisfied with the client experience they receive because they are looking for salespeople who aren't simply order takers. They are looking for that fourth category of salesperson I described earlier. A salesperson who knows the industry trends, and can prove in a conversation with a CIO or CEO that they understand the pressures their business is under, and can tailor the solutions they are selling accordingly.

Account Plans

Account plans today are created by the salesperson attached to the client. They are a current snapshot of data or facts such as the executive structure, the operating plan and the footprint of the client organisation and so on. This information is mostly cut-and-pasted from the web page of the client. Indeed, if you went to the client's webpage, I'd argue you would find all of the same data that's in today's account plans in more detail, easier to navigate and better laid out.

Field Marshall Helmuth von Moltke, the Elder, of the great Prussian Army in the 1800s, famously said, and I'm going to paraphrase this: 'Your battle plan and your battle strategy are all very well until the first shot is fired. Then everything goes out the window.'

Account plans can function like that today. In the case of the first shot fired, the shot is an opportunity. Once an opportunity from the client comes along, typically the account plan is dropped and the client is chased. Mainly because, given the account plan is a snapshot of the current time, they aren't helpful in securing the opportunity that lies in the future. The account plan today is usually devised at the start of the year, and I've worked in organisations where the salespeople are actually paid to write these plans, only to have them put away in a drawer until the following year. That's how useful they are.

Account plans need to address the future. I'll use the analogy of the best soccer players in the world who seem to be able to see into the future and anticipate where the ball lands, they aren't simply chasing it. Account plans need to include the global, national, and regional trends of the industry their clients are in, and predict, like the best soccer players in the world can, where the ball will land, or where the client wants to position their business in the future. These predictions aren't always going to be right, but, even if they're not entirely correct, this predictive view of the client is much more useful than the view in account plans today.

For example, we might have a client where we predict that for them to be competitive in three years' time, they are going to need to look at their business processes and introduce robotic-process automation. The client, in their purchasing plans and in their current go-to market, doesn't actually have that annunciated, which isn't to say they aren't thinking about it. Clients are smart and they will be looking to the future and they will be wanting to have conversations around how that looks, so we, as experts in the field, need to begin those conversations before our competitors. We need to be selling to this long-term goal. We will have other opportunities that arrive along the way, but we must continue to pursue this long-term prediction.

That's the level of insight we need to get into account plans today. To do this, we must have a comprehensive understanding of the market, the evolving offerings, and of the client. That's not to say that you sit down with the client on day one and tell them that they will need to introduce robotic-process automation into their business in three years' time. These conversations need to be built one step at a time. It's that long-term view of the client in the account plan that will shape the conversations we have with them today and will, over time, enable those longer-term conversations and deals.

Account plans also need to contextualise the future and look at least 36 months ahead. I will go into more detail on this when I describe Attainment Plans later in this book.

For example, you might have a client who is operating in five countries today. Their strategic imperatives prescribe they want to operate in 10 countries in three years' time. Between now and then, they are either going to need to establish operations from scratch, or acquire a company in those countries and change the label on the building, or establish a joint venture. All of these scenarios are really valuable to consider because, as the client's overall strategy changes, so must the sales approach, and being prepared for these changes is important.

Account plans today can't accommodate that strategic vision because they are only developed every 12 months. I know that for any CEO a 36-month account plan is a big cultural shift, but if it's a realistic plan that has the elements I'll talk more about later in this book of credibility, capability, commitment and control, then it's a powerful shift that will make sense — especially if there's a $100 million deal attached to it.

Especially when this deal has been identified as the one mega deal that you have a likely chance of winning, following a robust process of evaluation. And you have a team of people working on this deal who have established 3-, 6-, 12- and 36-month goals with the client. And the entire team has bought into the account plan because they created it together from the very beginning and they review it every week. And over time, you see that the team is meeting the shorter-term goals with the client. And there's an over-arching belief statement that unites the sales team and aligns it with the client. Then, as the CEO, you're going to tick off this 36-month approach because you're very confident that you're doing the right work that will position you to land a $100 million deal at the end of it.

Overlay Targets

There is nothing good about overlay targets. They shouldn't exist. Most overlay targets are set for what we call 'specialist' salespeople. An IT organisation might have a cloud specialist, or a security specialist, or a software-licensing specialist, or a maintenance specialist. You name it.

I'd argue that the only reason specialist salespeople have evolved is because our sales teams aren't performing as they should. That's not to say that we don't need specialists, but they just shouldn't be tied to the sales team. I'll be going into more detail in The Right Team section later in this book.

Overall, the sales team should be learning the offerings better, rather than deflecting responsibility for this by saying something along the lines of: 'Oh, security's too specialised for me, so we need to bring in a specialist security salesperson.' The fact is, specialists in the sales team should not exist, but they do, and these sales specialists are given overlay targets. These targets don't flow through to the bottom line, they are simply incentives for the sales specialists to perform. The only targets that do flow through to the bottom line are those given to the salespeople.

For example, the CEO, after sign-off from the board, has said to the market, 'We're going to turn over $100 million this year.' The CEO then gives the sales manager a target of $110 million. The sales manager then hands out $120 million to the six salespeople in the organisation at $20 million each.

Knowing that only 20% of the sales team will get their number, the CEO and sales manager have increased the target the CEO went to the market with in order to build in some safety. There might be three specialist salespeople and they are also each given a target of $20 million. If I am the security specialist salesperson in this scenario, and I've heard that one of the other salespeople is having a conversation with a large bank on a $20 million deal, and $5 million of that is security, then I'm going to scramble to get involved in that deal so I can be tagged for that $5 million.

This completely drives the wrong behaviour. It is utterly and solely opportunistic. The specialists are jumping all over the place trying to get themselves into every single deal, arguing that they've sent emails to the clients and have attended client meetings so they can get tagged.

The client is confused by the veracity of the sales specialist's interactions. The salespeople become resentful because they feel the specialist is stealing recognition for the deal, or the specialist hasn't contributed enough from the beginning to even be associated with the deal. And, in some cases, the salesperson is fighting against the specialist being tagged in the deal because it will take a portion out of that salesperson's commission. They will lose as much as 20% of their commission to the specialist salesperson. This can happen in reverse as well, where the sales specialist has landed the deal and the salesperson is jumping up and down trying to become a part of it so they can grab some commission.

Here's one real-life example of overlay targets in action. I was involved in a $54 million deal that we won, of which about $12 million was for security. It was a long process over many months and we had roughly 60 meetings with the client. Our sales security specialist turned up to only one of these meetings and claimed the entire $12 million security portion of the deal because of that. Management awarded it to them.

This led to anger and resentment within the sales team because it was clearly wrong. The culture within the sales team was completely destroyed overnight and it took many months to repair. Yet it was within the rules. I think, in this case, it was also a poor call from management given the justifiable response from the sales team, but the real problem was the overlay targets and a lack of sales leadership.

I'm going to say it again for emphasis. Overlay targets should not exist in our industry and I am yet to meet a COO or CEO who disagrees with me on this. The question that always follows is: 'But what else can I do, Andrew?'

4. Our CEO

Everyone who works in an organisation plays a critical role or they wouldn't be employed. Most of these roles are what I call 'doing' roles. They could be in accounting or sales or delivery or a professional service — all of these things. These roles, either independently or combined, achieve results by doing pieces of work. They are roles that sit within the structure of the organisation.

It is the CEO who sits at the top of this structure. They are the face of the organisation and they drive confidence into the market. This is what I call a 'being' role. The CEO doesn't necessarily describe what needs to be done; they describe the cultural and ethical standards of the organisation. They project the image of the organisation by setting the behaviours that are and aren't accepted, and the standards that are passed, or not passed. The CEO is the focal point of the organisation simply through being. Of course, they also do things, but the being is a key function.

It isn't the most important thing a CEO does today, though. Their most important function is to accept and deliver the numbers. The numbers are predominantly the overall revenue figure and the profit within that figure that the board and CEO have agreed to over a 12-month period. This is what the shareholders have staked their investment upon. Today that is the key measure of success for any CEO: to drive shareholder value.

For example, the board has said the market is growing at 7%; therefore, the CEO must grow the revenue of the organisation at 7% to meet market expectations, so the share price will remain stable. On this basis, the number is set and then, as I've described earlier, that number is essentially added to and divided, then given out across the organisation as sales targets. I might be over-simplifying, but that's essentially the type of conversation which is being had in organisations today.

For the record, I completely disagree that the most important function of the CEO is to drive shareholder value. Shareholders are anonymous and they come and go, focused solely on making money from the organisation. Obviously, making money, at the end of the day, is what we all want, but to make it solely for shareholder value drives bad behaviours.

For example, if towards the end of the financial year the organisation doesn't have enough revenue and profit, they will look to take costs out of the business to maintain profit, thereby lowering their service level to clients. In the short term, this might increase the dividend for the shareholders, but in the long term it could mean the loss of clients. And once this revenue — which was derived from those lost clients, and the margin associated with them — is taken out of the organisation, then the shareholders will no longer see value in the organisation and they will leave as well. It's a lose-lose long term.

I believe the most important function of the CEO should be to deliver value to their clients. If an organisation helps their clients achieve their goals over the short term and into the longer term, then those clients will remain with the organisation over that long-term period. This in turn will drive revenue and profit for the organisation long term, which in turn will deliver shareholder value. By focusing on the client, the shareholder also wins, which isn't the case the other way around.

Or putting it another way the CEO should be owning and driving stakeholder leadership:

Stakeholder Leadership

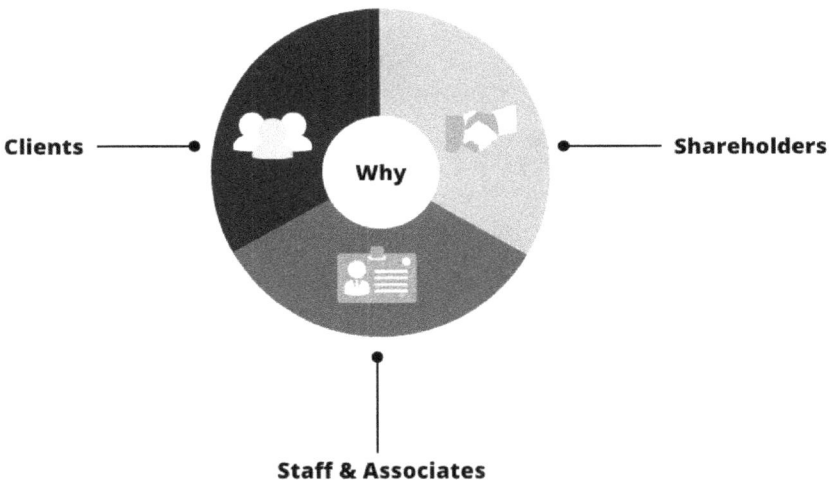

Clients — Why — Shareholders

Staff & Associates

In stakeholder leadership there are three primary stakeholders: clients, staff and shareholders. I'd still argue that the clients need to come first, but there needs to be a strategy that addresses all three stakeholders.

So given this focus today on shareholder value, the question that concerns most CEOs on a day-to-day basis is ...

As the CEO, Am I 100% Confident We'll Achieve Our Numbers this Year?

CEOs are primarily occupied throughout the year with two numbers: the total size of the pipeline and the current year-to-date achievement. The industry rule here is that the pipeline coverage must be three times the target number, and then there's a reasonable expectation that the target number will be achieved. I say reasonable because in reality this three-times coverage is really just an estimate that has built up in the industry over time and seems to be true most, or at least some of the time. In reality, this pipeline coverage number means little if it isn't interrogated.

For example, you might have a target of $100 million with $400 million in the pipeline, which is higher than our three-times coverage, so as a CEO you might be fairly confident in hitting the number. Within this $400 million pipeline there might be five deals, of which one is worth $300 million and the other four are worth $25 million each. The pipeline has more than three-times coverage, but really you're sweating on one mega deal and there's nothing, given this level of coverage, that's sounding alarm bells.

The CEO might be happy under this situation to report to the board that they have good pipeline coverage, and that the numbers are going to be reached without once examining the likelihood of winning that one mega deal. It's possible in this scenario that the likelihood of winning that deal is extremely low, but the salesperson doesn't want to come clean with the CEO, as that would wreck the entire year, and they are still hanging onto whatever hope there is left.

There's an expression: *It's easier to ask forgiveness than it is to get permission.* In this case, the salesperson isn't seeking permission to change the numbers, but they will be eager to ask forgiveness after the fact. The salesperson might also be bidding the business, rather than creating it. They may only be quantifying the deal, rather than having long-term strategic conversations with the client to position themselves to win the deal. And sure, they may also be praying for a bluebird, which does happen — those deals that come in out of the blue. But relying on these factors is like relying on the roll of a dice.

I've never worked with a CEO who was 100% confident in the numbers. And in reality, I don't think under any system it's possible to have 100% surety, because even if you're the best-placed provider for the client and have effectively agreed to all the deals to make up the numbers, the market and the client can change suddenly and unexpectedly.

I would, however, argue that most CEOs have little to no confidence in the numbers, because a considerable number of them today are having failing conversations with the board at the end of year. They are asking for forgiveness because they didn't make their numbers. As are the sales managers reporting up to the CEO. It's a systemic issue. I've certainly never worked with a salesperson who was anywhere near 100% confident they were going to hit their sales number. I've even been that salesperson.

A few years ago, I was VP of sales and I had a number of sales managers reporting up to me. I had little to no confidence in the numbers because our conversations went something like this. I'd ask: 'When's the next sign-off for that deal?' I'd get an answer like: 'I don't know, but it's going to close this quarter.' To which I'd reply: 'It's going to close this quarter, but you don't know what day the next sign-off is?' To which they'd reply: 'Yeah, that's right.'

Or I'd ask: 'Who's the sponsor on the board for the deal?' To which they'd reply: 'I don't know.' To which I'd ask: 'When are they going to place the order?' To which they'd reply: 'Oh, the guy's on leave.' It became embarrassing and in some circumstances I stopped asking questions. It was no different to the school teacher asking after homework that the dog ate.

My salespeople happily reported scenarios that were completely devoid of reality. We did, however, mostly scrape through at the end of the year, and made our numbers, which came down more to luck than planning.

The real question, therefore, is that if our CEO doesn't have 100% confidence in the numbers, because this isn't realistic, then what is the ideal confidence level to have? This will, of course, vary throughout the year and really depend on a number of factors.

I think the ideal level of confidence to have is that you are 100% confident you're being told the truth. This is the only way to increase confidence in the numbers. Right now I guarantee that every CEO in the market has a multimillion-dollar deal in their pipeline which is already dead. A dead deal isn't one that is necessarily lost, but it's a deal that never even existed.

For example, I might be talking to a client and suggest we replace a portion of their infrastructure. They might get excited by this, and we might have further conversations which are great conversations to have. The deal might be worth $20 million and I'm desperate for pipeline coverage this year, so I put it in the pipeline at $20 million even though I probably know it's a deal that won't mature this year. There are many things that need to occur that realistically will take years. And this happens all the time. It is simply an idea at this point that should never have been put in the pipeline for this year.

If, however, the CEO was told the truth, then that deal could be taken out and the focus could shift to the deals that can be won. There might be levers to pull to move these other deals further up into the likelihood of success, levers that aren't currently being pulled because the focus is on the deal that is already dead. Essentially, the truth will allow better decisions to be made to win the deals that can be won.

For example, I was commencing a new role at the time and my team had a target of $100 million for new business acquisition. We had 16-times pipeline coverage, well above the generally accepted three times. From the outside, you'd expect us to be really confident in hitting our target. Yet over half of this pipeline was taken up by one mega deal.

This deal had been in the pipeline for two years. The CEO was in love with this deal. Another deal took up about half of the remaining pipeline. So over three-quarters of the pipeline was taken up by just two deals. The remaining quarter of the pipeline was spread across half a dozen smaller deals. I would do a forecast, and with the understanding of how the smaller deals were progressing, I believed we would probably hit just below our target for the year, which we did in the end.

The following year's planning was underpinned again by this mega deal, as it was back in the pipeline. This strategy of recycling everything back into the pipeline is fraught with danger, because from the outside everything looks really positive. The pipeline dashboard is lit up green like a Christmas tree, but really it's in the red — nuclear red. I left the organisation that year. The mega deal was lost and there weren't any of the smaller deals won, which left the entire forecast in tatters. Now, obviously, it wasn't just the forecasting mechanism that failed here. There were other structural issues that were reflected in that lack of performance.

The real challenge for CEOs today is that they can't simply go back to the board and say: 'I'm not going to make my number this year.' They then transfer this pressure onto the salespeople by telling them that they must make their number without fail. The sales team then fill their pipeline with every deal they can, so at the very least they can say to their manager, or to the CEO: 'Yes, I have three-times pipeline coverage.' And even if the salesperson knows deep down it's never going to materialise, they only have to wait until the end of the year for the number to be reset. Phew! As long as they've kept their job, they have another shot.

Meanwhile, the CEO is gradually losing credibility with the sales team, especially those 75% we discussed earlier that aren't going to make their number, because they feel the CEO should be going back to the board to be more realistic with the numbers. The majority of the sales team are then having more healthy conversations with recruiters than with their clients — selling themselves better to the recruiters than they ever sold the offerings of the organisation they are currently working for.

And when I've interviewed potential sales hires, I have to say that I have never interviewed a single salesperson who hasn't made their number every single quarter of every single year. The result of all this is obviously that no one is telling the truth. I've been made aware of situations where the sales team has missed their numbers, yet the CEO has been rewarded for great performance because the numbers that the CEO handed out to the sales team were far above theirs. Obviously, if the sales team finds out about this, then it can have an adverse effect on both morale and culture.

Ultimately, I believe CEOs need to change this paradigm. They need to stick their head out and say: 'Currently the system isn't working. We need to try something different because we want to build a stable organisation that delivers long-term success for our clients, our people and our shareholders/owners.' As I've said previously, any change to the current system can't happen overnight, it will take time. But I guarantee the CEO who undertakes and commits to this change will stand out in the marketplace, mainly because they will be the organisation winning most of the deals. They will be the organisation making their numbers every year — the organisation everyone wants to work for.

Inside the Board Meeting

Boards, whether advisory for non-publicly listed organisations, or legally bound in the case of publicly listed organisations, can play a really positive role. The ideal board in my opinion is one that has a diverse set of skills across its personnel and takes a balanced long-term strategic view for the organisation. An ideal board isn't shareholder centric, but considers, in equal measure, the three major stakeholders I've outlined previously: clients, staff and shareholders. It is a board that lifts the CEO into the future, energising them to put that long-term strategic vision into operation. It is a board that is inquisitive about the future and asks 'what if' questions like: 'What if we were able to do this in the marketplace, what would happen? Where would that take us?'

It is worth viewing the role of boards through the prism of Simon Sinek's Golden Circle diagram from his book *Start With Why*.[3]

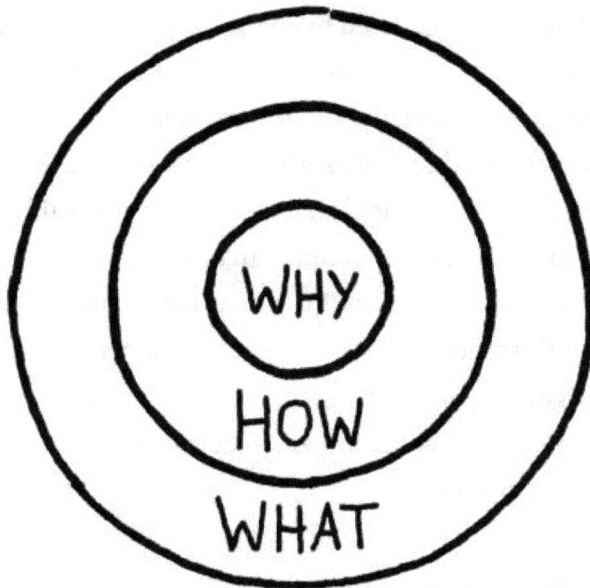

An ideal board will also explain *Why*, which is the purpose and reason for their strategy. *Why* is often overlooked in business broadly.

---

3   The Golden Circle diagram is reproduced from the book *Start With Why* by Simon Sinek (2011) and is reproduced with the permission of Penguin Random House, UK.

For example, I might tell you over and over to cross the road. This is *What*. Are you going to do it? Maybe. But if I explain *Why* you need to cross the road — perhaps because there's a hungry lion on this side of the road that won't eat you if you cross to the other side of the road — then you are going to cross the road quickly, because you understand *Why* you need to do so.

The ideal board not only explains *Why* but they also explain *What*. What is our long-term strategy to get to where we need to be in the future? An ideal board will operate predominantly in the *Why* and *What* bands and be less involved in the *How*. Which is *How*, as an organisation, do we put the long-term strategy into place?

The board must still be aware of the *How*, particularly where ethics and transparency are concerned, but be less hands-on here. The *How* is predominantly the job of the CEO. And, of course, an ideal board operates within and meets all the required legal framework. This is the ideal board in my opinion, a board I'd describe as progressive.

Boards too often today become blinkered, like the organisation itself, with the 12-month sales cycle. Early in the year, the board may be optimistic, looking forward to making the numbers that have been set for the organisation. And over time, they tend to ride these numbers, so, if suddenly the numbers begin to look out of reach, they are asking operational questions around how the shortfalls can be made up. Or they are increasing the pressure on the CEO to deliver the numbers, which can set up an adversarial relationship. Or they are looking at how costs can be taken out of the organisation late in the year, if the numbers are still falling short.

Boards can also get fixated on inputs or the day-to-day activities of the organisation, rather than outcomes based on the implementation of the strategy.

So, if I'm a CEO in a board meeting, then I'm running through the pre-agreed business metrics (the numbers). I'm explaining any abnormalities, whether negative or positive. And, of course, these metrics are all in the past, they are history, they have happened, there is nothing that can be done to change them.

The only real view of the future is the pipeline, which as we've already discussed has a large degree of inaccuracy. As a CEO I may have contributed to this inaccuracy by taking a third of the value out of the pipeline, because I'm only around two-thirds confident in the picture my sales manager has painted. My numbers might fluctuate dramatically between meetings, which comes back to strategy.

If the strategy is to develop a large number of new clients every quarter, then my numbers are going to fluctuate more than if the strategy is to retain long-term clients. Each strategy has its strengths and weaknesses and ideally, as a CEO, I'm presenting my numbers with a mix of both long-term clients and new clients for growth, and I'm explaining the number fluctuations this way.

If I am a CEO with a progressive board, then I know there will be scrutiny around the numbers, but the board won't fixate on the numbers solely. We'll also be having really interesting, even inspiring conversations about the future. Most likely though, I'm a CEO who doesn't have a progressive board and we're getting bogged down talking through the numbers, looking for shareholder return. I'm concentrating on the past (the current numbers) and a skewed view into the future (the pipeline) and, at the end of it, as a CEO, I'm left without any real guidance as to how to tackle that future.

I've also most likely got a sales approach that's stuck in the past with three indicative symptoms that essentially function as poorly designed band-aids, which have completely eroded any confidence I have in the numbers or in the pipeline: overlay targets, the transactional sales manager, and was your last year saved by one deal?

Overlay Targets

I've covered overlay targets for sales specialists in the previous section and explained how I think overlay targets shouldn't exist. Specialists are necessary, but they shouldn't have these individual sales targets assigned to them because they have the potential to drive individualistic behaviours in the sales team. The distinction to be made here is that specialists are necessary, sales specialists with overlay targets assigned to them are not.

Yet as a CEO today, when my sales manager comes knocking on my door to sign off on recruiting a new sales specialist, I'm torn between enabling and supporting the sales team and the need to manage my P&L. If I decide to support them, then I'm placing a bet on them reaching their target for the year with this additional resource. This alone highlights the structural flaw in the sales team today that I alluded to in the previous section. Sales teams today become reliant solely on individuals. Because there's no team built around the salesperson, then all I have, as the CEO, is their word, and their word alone. I'm also probably thinking that if our numbers for the quarter are looking poor and I need to strip costs out of the business to save the share price, then these sales specialists are the first people I can show the door, because, as I've explained, their overlay target isn't attached to the 'real' target.

So, as a CEO, I see these sales specialists as expendable, as a necessary then unnecessary cost. Now if I hire salespeople who are intelligent, nimble and have a thirst for knowledge. Who want to know enough about the specialist areas to have a great conversation with a client CEO about them. Who have a long-term strategy with their clients and understand where their value proposition lies in each of their offerings. And these salespeople are out there, which makes specialist salespeople an expendable and unnecessary cost.

And whilst we're on the subject of sales specialists, I'd like to mention vendor-funded sales specialists. These are cancer for any organisation today because these specialists only focus on one thing: selling their own vendor solutions. They spend all their time trying to influence both the organisation to sell and the client to buy their vendor's solutions, regardless of whether their solutions are the best fit or not. By definition, this is as far removed from selling those particular solutions — no matter who the vendor is — that perfectly fit the client's long-term strategic imperatives.

Further, these vendor specialists don't add a single dollar to the sales target, and resources need to be spent to manage them. In my 20-plus years in IT, I've never seen a successful vendor-funded salesperson. Initially, you might think this is great because they're free, but, ultimately, their priorities are different to the organisation's and they do little else but interrupt and distract the sales team from what they should be focused on: good client outcomes.

The Transactional Sales Manager

The transactional sales manager spends most of their time busily preparing sales reports for the CEO. They also manage the sales team, which invariably, with this type of manager, comes down to ensuring the sales team fill in their CRM alongside managing their account and sales plans. This is essentially holding the salesperson's hand. The transactional sales manager spends 80% of their time on transactions and 20% on coaching.

The transactional sales manager loves to be invited to client meetings because they don't have enough trust in their salespeople to construct the conversation alone. They are also reactive to what's going on, so they think that by attending meetings they are adding value when, in reality, because they don't know the client, they are detracting from that value. Ultimately, they believe they can provide the three magic words needed to close the deal.

The transactional sales manager needs to be completely removed from all organisations. Ultimately, there's nothing that a transactional sales manager does that good salespeople can't do for themselves. Essentially, many organisations are paying six-figure base salaries to transactional sales managers to run the numbers and ensure the sales team, who are also on six figures, fill in their CRM. As a CEO, you've got to look in the mirror and say: 'I'm seriously paying someone six figures, and then I'm paying someone else more than that a year for that person to scrub their pipeline for them? And I'm happy about it?'

If, however, that transactional sales manager was freed, and capable of doing things that make a difference sales-wise, then I would feel different about keeping them in the role. If they became a strategic Sales Coach to help guide the sales team and their approach to selling, to help change the outcomes, then that would be worthwhile. They would need to be significantly freed from running the numbers which — if the salespeople are updating their CRM accurately with opportunities, and that is being fed directly to the CEO with transparency — could easily occur.

This increased transparency might scare some salespeople and sales managers out there, but the benefits of re-focusing the transactional sales manager's role on the art of selling would far outweigh the downsides. It would definitely have a much more positive impact on sales than running flaky numbers and holding the hand of each salesperson. This change would invert the time a transactional sales manager spent on coaching: 80% coaching, 20% transactional. Later in this book, I will go into more detail about the role I believe sales managers of the future need to take.

The transactional sales manager is widespread and has been with us for many, many years. They can also be called the hit-and-miss sales manager because invariably, and without warning, that's what happens. And whilst the board and the CEO will create a large amount of commotion around those years that miss, essentially, or eventually, they accept a miss as the norm. Mainly because once the end of year ticks over, everything is reset and the outcome of hitting rather than missing becomes the focus once more.

The biggest cost of this acceptance is that the ability of the organisation to predict future outcomes goes out the window. Because the truth is hidden in those three things: uplift targets, individualised salespeople and inaccurate pipelines, no one in the organisation truly knows the likelihood of hitting the targets in the coming year. This leads to reactionary cost-cutting behaviours in the years that miss to save the year for that one stakeholder that many CEOs and boards value above all else today: the shareholder. And if the year can be saved for the shareholders, then it needs to be, because any confidence of hitting the numbers in the following year just isn't there.

This reactionary behaviour comes at the cost of the other two, arguably more important, stakeholders: clients and staff. And as I've explained previously, once these two stakeholders suffer, then it isn't long before the shareholders suffer as well. And if the organisation misses a couple of years running, then the pressure on the CEO to deliver a hit grows and grows and grows and grows.

Was Your Last Year Saved by One Deal?

I've mentioned bluebirds — deals that come out of nowhere late in the year — and how, as salespeople, we often pray for these to come through and save the year for us. I'm not for one moment advocating that these aren't good deals to go after, nor that chasing deals on the last business day of the year isn't a worthwhile thing to do. As salespeople, we should always do our utmost to land the deal when the deal is due, no matter how the deal originated, whether it arrived during the year, or whether it dropped in at the last moment.

From my experience, many organisations today either get their number or miss it by a mile because of one individual deal. This is the deal that saves the year, and for the majority of organisations today their year is saved by this deal more times than it's lost. So most organisations today get their number most years, or are quite comfortable to reach 90% or 80% of that number because that one large deal comes through, often at the last minute. I hear you ask, that if that's the case, then why change?

The first problem with that deal saving the year is that it isn't predictable. It's a binary equation in that you either hit your number that year or you miss and, given the nature of these deals, the majority fall into the pipeline late in the year, so there's very little information to determine whether you can land the deal or not. There simply hasn't been enough time in the lead-up to plan and influence the outcome.

These deals are solely in the hands of the client and, inevitably, the salesperson hasn't spent those two or so years getting to know the client and learning their long-term strategic imperatives. Therefore, even the person closest to the deal can't reliably predict whether they will be successful or not. This uncertainty, or lack of predictability, as I outlined in the previous section, can lead to cost-cutting behaviours that negatively affect staff and clients.

The second problem is there's no measure in place as to whether that deal fits with your organisation's strategic vision. Those deals that move your organisation forward strategically to ensure your organisation transforms. If your organisation fails to do this, then you risk becoming your client's legacy provider, which opens your client up to your competitors when they are looking to transform.

For example, it could be a pure hardware deal; however, your organisation is looking in the long term to move into self-service, automation and analytics. But because the hardware deal is there and it could save the year, then you're doing everything you can to secure it. And when this deal isn't a fit with your organisation's long-term strategic plan, then inevitably you're lower down the list of vendors in the client's eyes because realistically you're probably not the best organisation in the marketplace to deliver that deal.

As a result of this, a third problem arises: because you're not the most suitable vendor in the client's eyes, the only lever you can pull to influence them towards you is price. You have to be the cheapest to get their attention and land the deal. And because you don't know the client well enough, you aren't certain which components of the deal can be stripped out. So instead of removing the components that don't deliver value to the client (i.e. removing costs to lower the price), you're keeping all the components in and lowering the price through discounting.

This discount comes directly out of profit. So you might land the deal to save the year, but the profit margin has come in second to the revenue. And it isn't until six months later, when the deal is in the delivery phase, that you work out whether it was a good deal or not. You might find that you're bleeding money and not achieving the deemed margin. You might even discover that you're losing money on the deal and you're left regretting landing the deal at all.

On top of this, if you're the salesperson working on that one deal that can save the year, then you're under extraordinary pressure from the sales manager to close the deal, because the sales manager in turn is under enormous pressure from the CEO, who in turn is under enormous pressure from the board.

In this case, if you're in the fourth quarter of the year and the deal hasn't closed, then the sales manager is asking you more than once a day questions like: 'What's the next step in the deal?' Inevitably, because it's a deal that's dropped late in the year, as a salesperson you haven't had time to develop a clear strategy or plan, to move the deal forward.

As a salesperson, you're in the luck stage and you're riding that luck as hard as you can. You're reassuring your sales manager — and I've been that sales manager — over and over that everything is going well. You're saying things like: 'The purchase order is sitting on X's desk ready to be signed.'

And when your sales manager gets sick of hearing this, he takes things a step further by asking something like: 'What's the name of the person who's making the decision on the next step of the deal? Have you spoken to them?' And as that salesperson, it's only a matter of time before you admit that you simply don't know who that person is.

There's bad behaviour on both sides here. A sales manager shouldn't need to know every little step, thereby illustrating their lack of trust in the salesperson. And the salesperson should know what the next stage in the process is. But in their defence, they engaged so late with the client that they couldn't possibly know what the next step is. It becomes a game like charades when everyone's running around making a lot of noise, acting like they're busily landing the deal and, because it happens year after year, they know their parts well. They also know that everyone else knows that it is just that: a game. But the focus is so intense everybody goes along with it.

A further problem, which I've touched on, occurs because all the focus from the CEO, the sales manager and the sales team is on this one deal. This means there's no room to focus on the next year, or the next year after that. All longer-term planning is on hold until this one deal is either won or lost. So this becomes the cycle. The organisation either wins the deal and gets their number or they miss, which, as I've outlined previously, becomes an issue only until the budgets are reset the following year. And once again, the ability of the CEO and the organisation to predict future success is completely lost. The organisation is planning for the worst and hoping for the best year after year after year.

There's a term organisations use today for a deal that can save the year: 'This is a must-win deal.' If you're in an organisation that uses this term, then your organisation suffers all or some of the problems I've outlined above. Your organisation isn't utilising a strong strategic-selling process. Defining a single deal as a 'must-win' takes resources and attention away from the other deals. In my opinion, for every single deal you go after, you must believe you can win, or you shouldn't be pursuing it. Of course, that's not to say you're necessarily going to win every deal.

Having said this, I do believe there's room to categorise deals. I use the term 'Bedrock Deal'. This is a deal that 100% fits the strategy of your organisation. The Bedrock Deal completely supports the vision the board has set as to where your organisation wants to position over the coming years. It is not the size of The Bedrock Deal that matters, it's the attributes of the deal that are important. Typically, they also affect the client's business processes. It might be a small deal relative to other deals, but the 'Bedrock' attributes within it make it more important. This is because these attributes are the ones that will lead your organisation into transforming and moving into the areas of the market in the future that are strategically important. It will set your organisation up for future success.

I've seen sales teams working back on the last night of the year, inputting deals to the system. When you're working for an overseas company, this can go into the morning of the day after because their year hasn't come to an end yet. I've seen sales managers on the phone at 10 pm on the last day of the year trying to win deals back that they've recently lost, and successfully doing so. I've had a vendor on one phone and a client on the other at the same time asking where their purchase order is — trying to get the deal across the line at the last minute. All of these things happen, and I'm not advocating putting a stop to these behaviours because deals can go down to the last minute.

The bottom line, though, is if you are coming in late to a deal and trying to win it at that last minute, then often you're competing on price and you're going to give up margin to do so. With long-term planning — getting to know your client and understanding their long-term strategic imperatives to better determine what is of value to them and what isn't — then you can win those same deals without rushing to the bottom on price.

You will then be in a position to blow the end-of-year number out of the water, because you've delivered significant value to the client that they are happy to pay extra for. I'm not saying this will happen with every single deal, you may still need to compete on price, but even in that case you'll know what costs to strip out of the deal without lowering the value in the client's eyes.

Sales Team Credibility

This section begins with a reinforcement of the equation I used earlier to illustrate the importance of credibility for a salesperson when dealing with clients:

Knowledge + Trust = Credibility.

This equation also applies to how your sales team members are regarded *within* your organisation. Does the sales team have credibility with the CEO?

Knowledge is proven when the salesperson understands their clients, understands the opportunities that their clients present, and can clearly articulate how these opportunities will help their clients achieve their goals.

Trust is proven when this knowledge is shown to be true, usually when these opportunities are turned into business.

If the organisation has a sales manager running the numbers between the sales team and the CEO, then it's clear to me that the sales team hasn't got credibility with the CEO. The CEO doesn't trust the sales team enough to go directly to the CRM. And if the CEO artificially increases the number they agreed with the board at the start of the year — handing it onto the sales manager — then that clearly shows the sales manager and the sales team lack credibility.

The sales team also lacks credibility with the sales manager because the sales manager is also placing an uplift on the target. This happens in the majority of organisations today, so it's true to say that both the sales manager and the sales team in most cases lack credibility with the CEO. And this becomes a two-way street: if a sales team lacks credibility with the CEO, then more than likely that CEO lacks credibility with the sales team.

When a salesperson is credible with a client, that client will want to have conversations about their future with this salesperson, and opportunities will come out of that. When a sales team is credible with a CEO, and a CEO is credible with the sales team, then that frees up the CEO to better understand what the future looks like for the organisation. The CEO can then start planning in detail for the organisation's long-term future, rather than worrying about the present, which is a very powerful position for a CEO to be in.

5. The Future

We've described how the market environment has changed and how the approach of the majority of organisations to the market has not. And whilst there is a disconnect between the two, and has been for many years, there are still organisations out there today that use a traditional sales approach and are successful. With a view to the future then, the obvious question for most CEOs is:

What If, as a CEO, I Do Nothing in the Future to Change the Organisation?

There are organisations out there today who can't change because they might be part of a larger group of companies that doesn't want to transform, or they might be a small subsidiary of a very large multinational. In these cases, the CEOs don't have the control, or the power to effect broad changes to the organisation. And without a doubt, like they are today, these organisations will continue to be successful into the future. They will succeed through driving their sales teams hard, through having significant buying power in the marketplace that enables them to discount deals and still make a margin, and through reacting to client requirements.

There are three major challenges these organisations will face in the future, which I have covered in previous sections. The first is that the performance of these organisations will become more and more unpredictable as they chase binary deals. This will lead to a loss of credibility in the market, and the organisation will then struggle to attract investment. The second is that through constant discounting, their margins and profit levels will come under increasing pressure. This will have a negative effect on staffing in terms of training, employing the right level of experience and having the right amount of resources when needed. And the third problem is due to their commoditised approach to the client and the inevitable pressures brought to bear by competing solely on price, their staff will be less engaged in the business.

The organisation is then unable to transform to meet their clients' future needs. Referring back to the stakeholder management diagram, staff and clients will suffer because inevitably these organisations gauge their success on shareholder value alone.

The organisations that are willing to change and adopt the solutions I will propose in the next part of this book will achieve the opposite effect. They will be more predictable, which will enable them to better plan for the future and think strategically. They will better adapt to the client environment and their clients' needs, which will enable them to build healthy margins and profits because they will build value with their clients, which their clients will be willing to pay for. And they will build a great reputation in the marketplace that will attract and retain talented staff.

There is one other distinction I'd like to make here, between organisations that are willing and able to change, and those that are not. An organisation that doesn't change is a management organisation, one that thinks tactically. If you're the CEO of a management organisation, then you are managing the organisation rather than leading it. You're spending all your time thinking tactically about the day-to-day running of the organisation. You aren't free to lead — to think about the future and where you'd want your organisation to be in, say, five years' time.

This, to me, also implies that the management organisation is performing badly. If it looks like the organisation isn't going to make their number for the year, then, as a CEO, my priority would be to focus on how to tactically improve this. Alternatively, if the organisation is performing well, then, as the CEO, I'm free to think about the future. I'm able to consider making changes to the organisation going forward. Ultimately, I'm leading the organisation, rather than managing it, which I'd argue is a much more powerful, satisfying and sustainable position for a CEO to be in.

I've used the word 'organisation' in the question beginning this section, because I believe change has to occur not only to the sales team but across the entire organisation. That's why this book is called *CEO-Led Sales*, because the entire organisation must calibrate their performance to sales, not just the sales team.

Is the Job, as a CEO Today, Becoming Harder?

I speak to a lot of CEOs who tell me that it is. They are finding the job is increasingly becoming tactical. They are riding their white horse in to save the day, day after day. In these cases, they aren't enjoying their jobs as they once might have, but for some of them, who are CEOs of their own organisation, they know they can't walk away. They certainly can't be shown the door. They have to stick it out and often they are getting more and more concerned about finding a way out of this.

The problem here is that, because they are thinking tactically, they aren't able to stop to think about or plan for the future. It becomes a tactical loop that is impossible to break out of. They are stressed because of the pressure they're under. They know they have to increase sales, so they're thinking about employing more salespeople; they are then looking at reducing costs elsewhere to afford those salespeople. Or they're pulling costs out of delivery resources which deliver poor outcomes for the clients.

Every CEO I speak to wants to break this cycle. They want to stop thinking merely months ahead and shift their focus into the future. They want to win the right type of deals that deliver a decent margin and move the organisation strategically forward. They just don't know, or don't have the bandwidth to contemplate, how they can achieve this. They are desperate for the solution that will not only make their job easier going forward but more satisfying at the same time.

Ethics and Transparency

For the majority of organisations today, ethics in the sales team primarily comes down to two things: don't lie to your clients and don't offer them bribes. Most salespeople today think if they adhere to these two things, then they are ethical salespeople.

I believe we have reached a point today where our clients expect more than this from sales organisations. This is in part due to the growing global trend that as a consumer you have the right to know. For example, as consumers today we want to know that the components of the things we buy are ethically sourced. We want to know that they were created free of child labour, in an environmentally sustainable way, and with positive social impacts for the workers involved. This transparency is becoming central to the purchasing decisions of consumers around the world.

This increased focus on ethics and transparency is also, in part, due to public hearings like the 2019 Royal Commission into the banking sector, where we learnt that the big Australian banks were putting profits above consumer needs through misleading and unethical behaviours.

I believe it is incumbent on all CEOs today to be transparent with their clients as to how the sales team will be remunerated. I believe it's the buyer's right to know what the seller knows. For example, if you're going into an electronics store to buy a laptop, then the salesperson's first question will be something like: 'What's your budget?' You tell them the budget and they will march you over to a laptop at that price. Now there might be three laptops at that price that will satisfy your requirements, but the salesperson led you to this one. Unbeknown to you, as the buyer, that's because the salesperson receives twice the commission on that brand of laptop.

I believe ethically, as the buyer, you should be told that. You should be told there are three laptops that meet your requirements, and on this particular one the salesperson gets double the commission. It's ethical because then, as the buyer, you can make up your mind knowing everything that the seller knows. It may not change your mind about which laptop to buy, or it may.

Ultimately, I believe when there's an imbalance between what the buyer and seller know, then it's an ethical imbalance. I also believe it's the job of the CEO to ensure that this imbalance doesn't occur.

It is the CEO who should be sitting down with their clients and having that conversation. Their conversation would outline the organisation's long-term strategy to explain why the sales team are incentivised to sell these solutions over other solutions. Explaining that this has all been calculated through careful market research and collaboration with the client, to determine that the solutions that are incentivised are the solutions that will deliver the best long-term outcomes for the client.

So the sales team will only receive a benefit when they deliver the best result for the client. The conversation should go further, because the client is very important, and outline the exact amount of money in incentives the organisation has placed on the client. I firmly believe this is the new level of transparency that is required today.

I also believe it will have two benefits. Firstly, it will build long-term clients. The CEO will build significant credibility with their clients by illustrating knowledge of their business and building trust through their transparency, which is integral to establishing those long-term client relationships I've already mentioned throughout the book. The second benefit is that fundamentally it is the right thing to do.

6. So Why Did I Write this Book?

In 2014 I was working as the Victorian general manager in a large IT company. I had just been given my target spreadsheet for the year and I was applying uplifts to it. We needed to increase revenue and gross profit across the board. In that moment, it struck me that there had to be a better way.

Sure, I had an idea around which areas to focus on, and was fairly aware of where we could grow, but rarely did I consider the clients, which was the very first lesson I learnt about selling. I was looking internally at the metrics the business needed to be successful, not externally at what our clients needed to be successful.

I closed down that spreadsheet, sat back and determined that I needed a strategy to address our clients' long-term success. That was the only discernible way I could look into the future to predict what the numbers would be with a much greater level of accuracy. I determined that I must be able to realistically create two-, three-, four- or even five-year pipelines. At the time we had an 18-month pipeline, which was essentially a dream line for all the reasons I've mentioned previously in this book.

I made a promise then and there that I would draw on all of my experience to improve that approach. That I would look for a new way to predict success, rather than putting a number on top of another number on top of another number, then hope for success.

Admittedly, this light-bulb moment came after a series of light-bulb moments. I noticed every year I was there that we had big deals in our pipeline disappearing with little explanation. We had uplifts being put on every number in an attempt to protect the business. Meanwhile, the complexity of the environment in which we were competing was increasing. I also realised I was being paid to be a leader, but mostly I was managing. And all the best minds in the organisation weren't focused on improving the IP (Intellectual Property) of the organisation by hiring the right people, finding the right clients and winning the right deals — we seemed to be only focused on laying off the risk.

So, in truth, I had all these light bulbs go off, one by one by one, to tell me that the system was broken and it was painful for people to manage, and it was painful for people to work in. It was also painful for boards and the executive to look at. Very little has changed since then. And everybody involved intrinsically knows the system is essentially broken, but that's the way it's evolved over many years, which means it requires the utmost determination to change it. That became my mission. The reason for this book.

*   *   *

So what happened in 2006 at the large systems integrator after we lost $20 million of our $43 million turnover?

As I said, we went back to what I knew. What I had previously learned as a police officer and a dive-store manager and in my early days in selling. That if everyone is focused on what their customers need to achieve, then we will deliver better service leading to our customers being more successful; and if our customers are more successful, then we will also be successful.

That was the first thing we did. We looked at every customer on our books and formed a view of what they needed to achieve to be successful into the future from what we were delivering to them at that time. If we weren't delivering the very best that could possibly be delivered to them, then we changed to make sure that we were. This wasn't a growth strategy to replace the $20 million we had lost; it was simply to shore up the business we had. To ensure we were stable, not sinking.

The second thing we did was to create a common understanding plan that enabled everyone in the organisation to understand where they fitted into the organisation. We called it 'The Plan for Success'. We fitted everyone in the organisation into seven functional categories. We gave everyone behaviour-based goals. Success for each member of the organisation was based upon successful behaviours, and what success looked like.

For example, for someone in sales, there was nothing in the plan for success about achieving their number, creating account plans, or updating their CRM. These are all inputs. We put outputs in the plan for success, for example: respond to your clients that same day; become a student of the industry; and proactively contact your clients to educate them on market trends. We knew that these behaviours would create more value for our clients and for our staff than the inputs. We also knew it was the creation of this value that would begin to drive change in the organisation.

I sat down with every single staff member and talked them through this plan one-on-one or in small groups. This empowered everyone in the organisation because they knew exactly what they had to do to be successful. They also knew, because this was done with 100%

transparency, what everyone else in the organisation had to do to be successful.

For example, it enabled the professional-services people to see clearly what the salespeople needed to do to be successful. The professional-services people could then change their activities in a way that helped the sales team become more successful, and vice versa. Quite simply, if you tell everyone in an organisation what they need to do to be successful, and how they link in with everyone else in the organisation, then that creates common purpose, empowerment and the ability to act completely independently of the organisation when needed. All of these things increase productivity. It also helped to create a really cohesive working team. This wouldn't have been possible without the great people around me who were prepared to go on this journey with me.

The third thing we did was to identify the new clients we had to win to grow the business. We started by looking at what we were doing really well with our existing clients that we could tailor to deliver to a new client. We knew through this process that we could prove to a new client that we could deliver exceptional value in those areas because we were already doing it.

So what happened?

It worked. We won new clients and the business continued to grow year on year. I left about six years later, when the business had a turnover of $140 million.

PART C:
THE SOLUTION

7. The Right Model

THE RIGHT MODEL

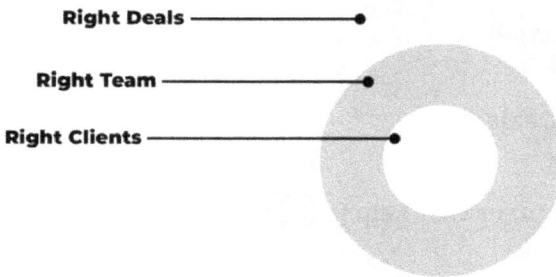

Right Deals ●————————●
Right Team ●————————●
Right Clients ●————————●

The Right Model is a model I have developed over time to support my learnings throughout my career. It is an organisational culture underpinned by a process. It's a culture of inquisitiveness, of urgency, of gaining and sharing knowledge, of engagement, of teamwork. I like to describe it as a culture that brings people together to form a collective 'battering ram'.

A battering ram will smash into a wall two times and, on the third time, it will likely break through that wall. By contrast, one sledge-hammer might smash against a wall 20 times and one swing might get through, but most swings barely make a dint. The wall in this analogy is The Right Deal with The Right Client. The battering ram is The Right Team smashing through to win it. The sledgehammer is the approach of most organisations today: sending one salesperson in at a time to win the deal.

The Right Model contains the:

- Right Clients

- Right Team

- Right Deals.

There are two plans that help to deliver each of these three things.

For **The Right Clients** there is the:

- CEO Sales Plan

- Attainment Plan.

For **The Right Team** there is the:

- Team Plan

- Remuneration Plan.

For **The Right Deals** there is the:

- Pursuit Plan

- Power Plan.

I will now go through each of these elements, in the above order, with the aim of changing the way you think about sales.

8. The Right Clients

THE RIGHT MODEL

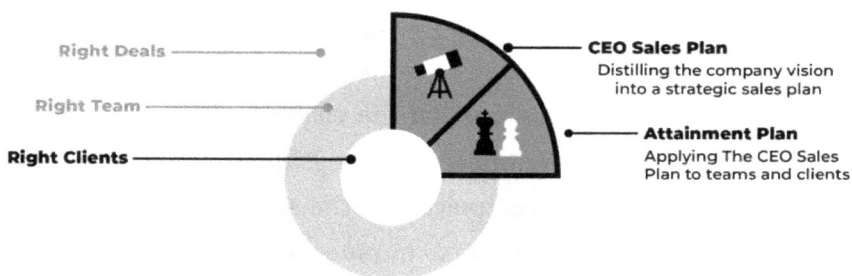

Right Deals

Right Team

Right Clients

CEO Sales Plan
Distilling the company vision
into a strategic sales plan

Attainment Plan
Applying The CEO Sales
Plan to teams and clients

The Right Clients enable your organisation to be successful because they are on the right or similar path to your organisation, have the right or a similar culture, and are growing at the right level. Quite simply, The Right Clients make it easier for you to be successful because they are headed in a similar direction to your organisation.

They also enable your organisation to evolve into those areas of the market that you, as the CEO, have identified will ensure future success for your organisation. The Right Clients aren't determined by the revenue they are currently delivering or will likely deliver; this determination is based solely on the compatibility of the journeys that the client and vendor are on. The more compatible the journeys, the higher the chances are for mutual success.

So how do we identify The Right Clients?

Through The CEO Sales Plan and The Attainment Plan.

The CEO Sales Plan

The Right Model begins with The CEO Sales Plan. The CEO Sales Plan is a strategic sales plan that the Sales Coach and the Client Experts implement into the future. (I go into more detail on Sales Coaches and Client Experts in The Team Plan.)

The CEO Sales Plan brings together the vision, the mission and the corporate plan of the organisation, alongside the challenges and opportunities in the marketplace and the solutions, services and technology that the CEO wants to pursue over a multi-year period. It also describes the attributes of the clients that the CEO has decided they want to pursue. The board delivers the strategic goals, but it is the CEO who steers the ship towards those goals. The CEO Sales Plan is the map.

I say 'multi-year' because the time period will vary according to the average contract term in your marketplace. For example, if the average contract term for those large deals that will fundamentally change your business is three to four years, then the CEO Sales Plan should cover that period. If the contract term is longer, for example, if your organisation builds major infrastructure projects like airports, then your CEO Sales Plan will need to cover a much longer period. It is designed to begin planning today to win transformational deals that come back to market in the future, or to be a disruptive force to bring those deals to market.

The CEO Sales Plan includes:

The 'Why' of the Organisation: This refers to Simon Sinek and his book *Start with Why* and describes the fundamental reason the organisation exists.

A Rallying Cause from the CEO: A statement that clearly articulates the direction in which the organisation is headed.

Core Beliefs: The rallying cause from the CEO, broken down into various beliefs that support that cause.

An Assessment of the Previous Year: Learning through a critical analysis of the past. This includes a look at things like the major wins in the past year and how they were affected by staff, the vendor and the client community. Questions will be asked:

- What do I wish I knew? For example, which major deal do I, as the CEO, wish I knew we were going to lose?

- What would I have done if? For example, what would I, as the CEO, have done earlier in the year if I knew we were going to lose that major deal later in the year?

- What worked last year?

- What didn't work last year?

An Assessment of Worthy Competitors: All competitors exist in an ecosystem. Worthy competitors are those that can leapfrog another organisation to win a deal. When this happens, the organisation that loses the deal learns from it. Ultimately, worthy competitors need to be embraced because they help an organisation to learn and grow. They add strength to the market and enhance client outcomes.

Solutions to Pursue into the Future: A list of solutions that the organisation will take to market now and into the future. An explanation of why these solutions are good for the organisation and what market forces are at play to ensure these solutions will be valued by clients. A description of the types of deals that would typically lead to one of these solutions being adopted by a client, and the types of competitors in that area of the market. These solutions must be drawn out into the future, looking at the readiness of the organisation to deliver them and how they will mature over time. It also includes a list of the key partners that will help deliver the solutions. Each solution is considered in detail with many questions that need to be answered. For example:

- What are the attributes of the target prospects?

- Which existing clients would be a prime target?

- Why is this good for our organisation?

- What market forces are in play that support our offering?

- Where are the prime reference sites?

- Who are the IP owners in our organisation that own this expertise?

- What sets us aside from our worthy competitors?

- What is the target year to be ready for delivery?

- Who are our key partners for this solution?

When the solutions are identified and drawn out over time, this will enable the Sales Coach and the Client Experts to translate these solutions into specific actions over a three- to five-year period. Conversely, this will also indicate those solutions that the organisation may want to exit in the future. An organisation only has a finite set of resources, so any pursuit of new solutions will inevitably lead to exiting others.

What Success Looks Like: A clear outline of success factors for the Sales Coach and the Client Experts, covering things like partnering strategies, Bedrock Deals, adhering to the Power Play and so on. This clearly guides the Sales Coach and the Client Experts towards long-term success.

The CEO Sales Plan is created by the CEO. This cannot be delegated, but assistance can be brought in. I say 'brought in' because I firmly believe assistance would need to come from outside the organisation to deliver the objectivity and independence required to help the CEO fully articulate all aspects of the plan. The fact that the CEO independently creates and owns this document is what makes The CEO Sales Plan completely different from any other plan that organisations put in place today. Of course, the CEO will turn to the key IP owners for input in creating the plan, but ultimately it's the CEO who owns The CEO Sales Plan.

Once created, The CEO Sales Plan must be revisited regularly and updated whenever there is major upheaval in the marketplace. The CEO Sales Plan is not another document to tick off each calendar year. It doesn't have a starting point, nor an end point. I'm a firm believer that business is a continuum: that once begun, it continues forever. Financial years and calendar years come and go but business never stops.

One mistake we often make today is to link our business planning to annual financial planning. The CEO Sales Plan will help disengage business from financial planning. Put simply, financial years work in cycles, opportunities with clients do not.

An example of a major upheaval in the marketplace that would require The CEO Sales Plan to be revisited would be the COVID-19 global pandemic of 2020/21. Over the eons, there have always been rises and falls in the marketplace. In this case, I'd suggest going back to the Global Financial Crisis of 2008 to look at what your clients did back then. More than likely, they will behave in the same way in 2020/21.

You might think about how, in the short term, you could transform your organisation based upon that. Alongside this, The CEO Sales Plan might contain a number of solutions that your organisation is going to transform into over the next four years. I'd suggest that, even with a major disruption like the COVID-19 pandemic, the long-term strategy wouldn't change. Another major upheaval might come internally. You may discover that one of the solutions or client segments you've chosen simply isn't working out, that you're not winning the deals like you thought you would. This would require The CEO Sales Plan to be revisited.

Ultimately, The CEO Sales Plan is a pragmatic view of all of the strategy documents that line organisations today. It distills the vision of the organisation into one actionable plan that a CEO can deliver to ensure that the organisation is headed in the right direction. It outlines the strengths, the weaknesses, the targets and the solutions for the organisation. Put simply it describes: what we're going to sell, the type of clients we are going to sell it to, and when we are going to sell it. It is a guide to success for all organisations.

The CEO Sales Plan identifies the attributes of The Right Clients. The Attainment Plan makes specific who those clients are.

The Attainment Plan

The Attainment Plan converts The CEO Sales Plan into an actionable working-territory plan for each Client Expert. It contains all the clients and all the deals that need to be pursued over the same multi-year period that The CEO Sales Plan covers. It contains a mixture of Stepping Stone Deals and at least one Bedrock Deal per client. Put simply, The Attainment Plan is the strategy document for each Client Expert outlining how they will be successful within their territory, with both existing and prospective clients that have the attributes contained in The CEO Sales Plan.

For example, the CEO Sales Plan might outline that the organisation will be investing in RPA (Robotic Process Automation). This investment will mature in two years' time and the attributes of clients needing this solution have been identified to have multi-state offices, over 200 staff, and are in the engineering, mining, retail or entertainment industries. The Attainment Plan will identify which current clients on the Client Expert's list have those attributes and which prospective clients need to be added to the list.

It will look at such things as which clients that have those attributes did our worthy competitors sign up three years ago on a five-year deal, which therefore will have a contract coming up in two years' time? In this example it gives the Client Expert two years to create the need in these clients for RPA. For some Bedrock Deals that timeline might be up to five years out. Over this time, some deals will come and go, that's just reality, but The Attainment Plan and The CEO Sales Plan will ensure the deals that are left are real, and identify the deals to replace those deals that are lost.

I've touched on the elements of a Bedrock Deal before, but I would like to reiterate that these are the deals that fundamentally change you and your target client. These are the largest (within the top 10%) and most profitable deals in the pipeline that hit straight into your sweet spot. They fully align with the direction the CEO has described the organisation will move in — in The CEO Sales Plan.

As I've said, The Attainment Plan ensures that each Client Expert is working on at least one Bedrock Deal with each of their clients because there's no point pursuing a client long term if they don't have a Bedrock Deal in their future. Most clients should have a Bedrock Deal in their future and, if they don't, then the Client Experts are perhaps not doing their job properly in identifying where the clients need to move in their future.

Either way, an organisation only has a finite number of resources, so you want to devote those resources to the possibility of winning a significant pay-off in the future. Bedrock Deals are often heavily services-led, with the bulk of the deal made up of professional services and managed services, with some supporting technology. Because of this service bias, typically the earlier you start with a client the more unique you can make your offering, which builds great value with the client that they are willing to pay for.

A Bedrock Deal is also fundamental to the business of the client, which means these deals have a high degree of visibility within the client, so the earlier you can start with the client, the more able you are to build the high level of support you need to win a Bedrock Deal. It will also present you with the opportunity to win one or two Stepping Stone Deals with the client. A client is highly unlikely to trust an organisation with a Bedrock Deal that is fundamental to their business operations that they haven't had some history with.

Some examples of deals that fundamentally change an organisation are fast-growth strategies like acquisitions or geographic expansions or new business models (i.e. a retailer creating an online channel to market). Other examples might be fundamental changes to the way the organisation does business, for example, replacing existing legacy systems or any other fundamental change to the core business systems of a client.

A Stepping Stone Deal is fairly self-explanatory. It is a small deal, for example: if your Bedrock Deal is, say, worth $15 million, then a Stepping Stone Deal might be worth less than $1 million. These Stepping Stone Deals should fit with the direction the CEO has outlined in The CEO Sales Plan. As I've alluded to, there might be a number of

Stepping Stone Deals with a client that help build credibility and trust with that client to enhance the chances of winning The Bedrock Deal.

Stepping Stone Deals also help an organisation decide whether to pursue a Bedrock Deal with a client. If that client hasn't purchased any Stepping Stone Deals with your organisation, then I suggest there's little chance you're in the running for The Bedrock Deal so, in this case, I'd walk away from pursuing that Bedrock Deal with them.

The Attainment Plan is written and owned by the Client Expert with coaching and guidance from the Sales Coach. It contains four core parts:

Attainment Plan

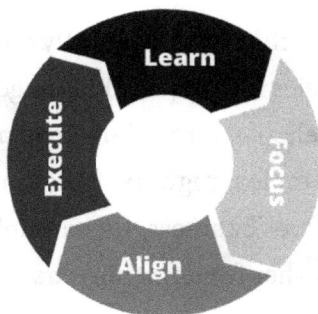

Learn:

This is similar to The CEO Sales Plan and focuses on what the Client Expert learnt in the previous year. It looks at who the worthy competitors were, who the partners were, and what they brought to the table. It reviews and interrogates how The CEO Sales Plan matches up with what has been learnt. It also critically reviews how knowledge was maintained of market trends locally, regionally and globally that affected each client. It also asks the Client Experts what is their 'Eminence'? Effectively, as they walk down the corridor of the office, what would they want everyone else to know them for? And why is that important to them? This helps the Client Expert focus their future behaviours, motivating them towards an ideal they have identified, that they want to own. It is akin to the CEO's rallying cause for the organisation applied to an individual.

Focus:

This identifies The Right Clients from all the things the Client Expert has learnt, both in terms of existing clients and prospective clients. It identifies the solutions the CEO has outlined the organisation must develop or move into during the next five-year period. It looks at a consulting strategy for the Client Expert to ensure they build trust and credibility with their clients. It also identifies those Stepping Stone and Bedrock Deals with each client.

Align:

This aligns four key components: the team, the partners, the clients and the reference sites.

Firstly, it aligns the team for client engagement. It looks at the strengths and weaknesses within the team and takes a view on how success can be achieved with the chosen clients based upon previous history with those clients.

Secondly, it aligns the best partners for the chosen solutions and determines how they will best support the sales effort and enhance the team.

Thirdly, it aligns the clients to the offerings. This is drawn out into the future by the Client Expert and Sales Coach using a target heat map that creates a matrix effect, which helps manage effort and resources. The real strategy here is to nominate when to begin to have those long-term conversations with the clients around the long-term solutions the organisation is offering, because the best solutions to be selling are the solutions that clients haven't started investigating themselves. If you can have those conversations, then you begin to own that solution in the client's mind. If the client is already well down the path of a deal, doing proof of concepts, or whatever, then you're too late to the game. These deals should be avoided, not because they can't be won, but because, as I've mentioned previously, these are the deals you're probably going to have to discount to win. And you're likely to be rushing your organisation to respond, and the scope is likely to get mixed up and profit levels will be challenged.

Fourthly, it aligns the reference sites to the clients for the Stepping Stone and Bedrock Deals. Reference sites are critical to winning deals. If you can prove you've delivered the same deal, in the same region and in the same industry as the client, then that can be a huge advantage over the competition. If you can take your client, who's thinking about doing the same deal you delivered to another client, to see that other client, and they say wonderful things about you and your organisation, then that's gold. Reference sites, of course, can be broken down. You might not have a reference site in the same region, but have one in another region; you may not have one in the same industry, but in another industry, and so on. If you don't have a reference site at all, then if your Bedrock Deal is four years away, you have time to land a Stepping Stone reference site deal.

Execute:

This covers client engagement, building credibility with the client and client expectations. It also assesses client behaviour: is this client behaving like a client who is going to buy a Bedrock Deal from us? It also looks at the outline for success in The CEO Sales Plan and describes the type of behaviours needed from the Client Expert to achieve fiscal success. An example of one behaviour might be to keep up with all the trends, disruptions and movements within your client's marketplace and clearly articulate this to the client when appropriate. Another might be to achieve the fiscal targets.

Like The CEO Sales Plan, once created, The Attainment Plan doesn't have a start or end date but operates, as the above diagram implies, on a continuum. It's the type of document that a Client Expert would pull out every Monday morning and say: 'Right, these are the things I said I was going to do. Am I doing these things? Am I living the process: learn, focus, align and execute? If the Stepping Stone Deal was lost last week, how can we get back on track for The Bedrock Deal?'

I'm not advocating that The Attainment Plan would need to be rewritten every week, just referred to and occasionally updated. As I outlined with The CEO Sales Plan, even with major market upheaval like the COVID-19 pandemic of 2020/21 the long-term strategy wouldn't likely change. Some short-term adjustments might need to be made, especially if there's a change internally, but over time the underlying basis of The Attainment Plan would remain.

The aspect that makes The Attainment Plan different from any other document I have seen in organisations today is it that it takes a multi-year view. It includes deals four to five years into the future, and has an inherent strategy on how to win those deals. It takes a fiscal view of those deals, which enables the organisation to create a realistic four- to five-year pipeline. This five-year view doesn't require extra head count, because The Attainment Plan enables Client Experts to become more targeted and effective with their time than most sales-people are today. Opportunities that need to be closed this year would likely take around 70% of a Client Expert's time, whilst 20% might go on deals for the following year, with 10% spent looking beyond that. And that's 30% more time than most organisations are giving those future deals today.

9. The Right Team

THE RIGHT MODEL

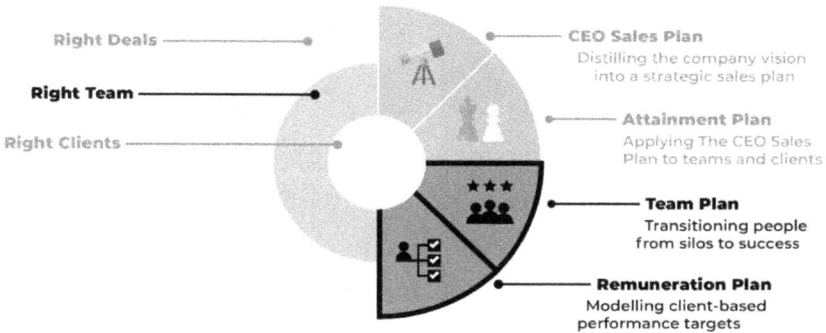

Right Deals
Right Team
Right Clients

CEO Sales Plan
Distilling the company vision
into a strategic sales plan

Attainment Plan
Applying The CEO Sales
Plan to teams and clients

Team Plan
Transitioning people
from silos to success

Remuneration Plan
Modelling client-based
performance targets

The Right Team brings a multi-disciplined, fully informed approach to the pursuit of Bedrock Deals. The Right Team is responsible for creating the strategy to win those long-term deals. The Right Team is especially powerful in the complex sales environment of today, which I outlined in the first section of this book, because they can demonstrate the number of different skills and capabilities to a client necessary to win Bedrock Deals.

This represents a huge advantage over the way deals are pursued today. Today it is mostly a single salesperson, and maybe an architect or specialist, who will consistently meet with the client in a long-term pursuit. It is then up to the salesperson to articulate back to the organisation the details and opportunity of the deal.

The disadvantage here is twofold: the client fails to see a large portion of the organisation's skills and capabilities; the salesperson and architect can't articulate back to the organisation the details of the deal as effectively as a multi-disciplined team can. These salespeople will bring in other people from the organisation at various points in the deal, but often these people lack the overall context of the deal because they haven't been involved from the beginning. Individuals simply don't have the same breadth of knowledge and insight as a team.

There will be a Right Team for every Bedrock Deal. The Right Team always includes the Client Expert and the Sales Coach and, ideally, four other members of the organisation chosen to bring a number of different skills and experiences that relate directly to the context of the deal. These members aren't in the team to do their day jobs, they are there to bring their unique perspectives, knowledge of the market and viewpoints.

For example, if The Bedrock Deal was to provide systems support for the client, then the head of HR would be a member of The Right Team. In this example, the client will primarily be concerned with three things: how well trained our people are, our staff attrition and staff engagement rates. These are not solely HR things, but they come out of an HR environment.

There is an enormous difference in credibility between a head of HR having a conversation with the client around 'How our organisation trains people,' and a salesperson saying something along the lines of: 'Oh, we have the highest level of staff engagement in our industry.' When you consider today there might be many other organisations competing for that Bedrock Deal, all sending one salesperson in to see the client, delivering similar sales messages, this difference is a very, very powerful competitive advantage.

This is *not* to advocate that the head of HR in this example would spend a lot of their time working on The Bedrock Deal. They would be in the team primarily to contribute to the deal's pursuit strategy that the Client Expert and the Sales Coach would spend the time driving forward. This might entail the occasional meeting with the client, but it wouldn't take over what they are there in the organisation to do, i.e. head up HR. I'd recommend that participation wouldn't take up more than 20% of their time.

The members of The Right Team are chosen by the Sales Coach with input from the Client Expert. The Sales Coach has to think broadly and laterally as to who in the organisation can bring the most value relative to the client environment. Members aren't necessarily chosen from the executive of the organisation.

For example, The Bedrock Deal might be in the transport industry and your organisation might have a storeman who worked in transport for many years. This storeman might be part of The Right Team to deliver really detailed insights into transport from the perspective of the challenges a worker faces at a grassroots level. These insights will prove invaluable when you're flavouring your conversation with the client CEO. You will be able to present a level of insight and detail from the worker's perspective that only the client CEO understands, which will go a long way to prove to them that you fully understand their business.

Members of The Right Team may have dual roles in the team. For example, you might have a legal representative on the team working on a Bedrock Deal in the media industry. This legal representative has been chosen because previously they held the position of chief legal counsel within a media organisation. Their dual role here will be to deliver extremely valuable strategic insight into the media industry based upon their experience alongside doing their day job, i.e. reviewing the Terms and Conditions (T's & C's) of the deal.

The Right Team would have a series of formal and informal meetings. Informal meetings would be ad hoc. The Client Expert might just wander down to a team member's desk to have a quick chat. Formal meetings would be quarterly, at most, if the deal was, say, five years off. They would be more regular closer to the deal closing. The timing of these more regular meetings would be determined by the moments in the deal pursuit when funding was required.

These meetings would be for The Right Team to apply The Power Plan, to run the lens of efficacy over The Pursuit Plan, to generate action points, to keep the deal pursuit on track. This will be fully explained when we reach The Pursuit Plan and The Power Plan sections.

The Right Team is remunerated on client outcomes, not on doing their day jobs. Bonuses will be paid, not only when deals are won, but also based on client success and on the team exhibiting The Right Behaviours. This is a big change to the way bonuses are paid today. Not only can salespeople under The Right Model be paid bonuses without landing The Bedrock Deal, other non-sales members of The Right Team can also receive bonuses. I will go into more detail on this in The Remuneration Plan section.

The Right Team brings multi-disciplined thinking to an opportunity to create the best possible pursuit strategy, alongside delivering transparency and accountability. The Right Team will hold each other to account to ensure that the action points that are created in the deal pursuit are followed up. The Right Team will collectively be able to determine the best deals to pursue, that the organisation has the best chance of winning, and those deals the organisation needs to walk away from.

This will enable the CEO to have greater visibility on the likelihood of winning deals because, unlike today where one salesperson's viewpoint is central to the conversation, The Right Team will deliver multi-disciplined, multi-viewpoint, fully informed and transparent analysis.

Right Team Example

Multi-discipline Team to support deal strategy

Sales Coach Guides strategy and approach

Client Expert

Client Expert drives activities and updates plans and CRM

Call Plans and Sales Actions developed and debated

Detailed Reviews and updates assessed against The Power Plan

The Team Plan

The Team Plan articulates how an organisation works together to pursue those Bedrock Deals identified in The CEO Sales Plan. It also fundamentally changes the approach most organisations take to selling today.

Organisations are broken down into many different areas. There's sales, delivery, managed services, finance, HR, legal, marketing and so on. All of these areas exist because they perform important functions. The Team Plan separates these functions into two areas: delivery and pursuit.

Delivery involves those areas that are engaged with the client around things the organisation has already sold to them. Delivery isn't covered by The Team Plan, but as one of the 4C's that I talk about later in The Power Plan; however, delivery is still a critical function that would be covered by existing bonus structures.

Pursuit is pursuing clients to win future business. Everyone else in the organisation, from the CEO through to the receptionist, falls into the pursuit area and will be covered by The Team Plan. The only minor exception here is you might have senior leaders in delivery who need to be included in pursuit and would be covered by The Team Plan.

This new approach ensures that everyone in the organisation who needs to be involved in a sale is included in a planned and structured way. This increases the effectiveness of the pursuit. Today, as I've previously mentioned, pursuit is primarily the realm of sales and perhaps an architect or specialist. The Team Plan incentivises and energises not just sales and an architect or specialist to sell, but most other areas of the organisation as well, which is a fundamental change.

To explain how this is achieved, I'm going to start with sales and then branch out. The Team Plan completely transforms traditional sales functions. Sales Managers will be replaced by Sales Coaches, and traditional salespeople will predominantly be replaced by Client Experts. This transition will be a gradual one, and the approach here would largely depend upon the skills of the current members of sales.

For example, if you have a Transactional Sales Manager who spends 80% of their time locked in their office checking that the sales CRM is up to date and that the sales team have delivered their forecasts, then that person probably doesn't have the skill set to become a Sales Coach. Alternatively, if you've got a Sales Manager who's spending 80% of their time developing their sales team through coaching and training, then they could probably very easily transition to the Sales Coach role. Therefore, The Team Plan would begin with a thorough evaluation of the skill sets that currently exist in sales. Those members who have the skill set to transition to become a Sales Coach or Client Expert could begin to do so immediately. Those who don't would still remain in the organisation doing their current sales roles.

A two-phase sales approach would need to be in place over a number of years to protect the current deals in the pipeline, and to also work on those small to medium transactional deals. These salespeople will still be performing important tasks for the organisation and will need to be developed and rewarded over time. This will make the implementation of The Remuneration Plan more challenging, but this approach will ensure the health of the organisation over the short to medium term.

It's also worth remembering that the Sales Coach, Client Experts and The Right Team are there to primarily work on Bedrock Deals

— those large deals that change the fundamental processes of your client and your organisation. Alongside these, there will always be those small to medium transactional deals that need to be pursued.

Often these deals will be Stepping Stone Deals. For example, The Bedrock Deal might be with a bank. At one end of this banking client, we are selling big strategic ticket items like applications development, transformational behaviours, cloud, data centre and robotic process automation; whilst at the other end of the sale, there might be headsets for their call-centre operators to wear. This deal to sell headsets wouldn't need to go through its own Pursuit Plan, it is a straightforward transactional sale. Obviously, this would be at the junior end, so you might find over time that you're actually employing entry-level people to manage these transactional sales.

The Team Plan would then look to develop and transition these new employees into Client Experts down the track. I've said this before, and I'll say it again, because I believe it strongly: it's always better to grow, transform and develop your current staff than to hire in all the time. The important point here is The Team Plan will retain and evolve your employees over time.

There are no hard or fast rules around the implementation of The Team Plan. Each implementation will be unique to each organisation. Each employee will be evaluated and given different paths and training to move forward. This is a long-term process. The fundamental point here is that you need to protect your current business whilst moving the business forward at the same time.

*   *   *

I've described some of the attributes of the Sales Coach role previously, but now I'll go into more detail. Sales Coaches replace traditional Sales Managers. The role of the Sales Coach is to constructively interpret and enable The CEO Sales Plan and ensure the company objectives are delivered. They work closely with Client Experts and The Right Team to ensure The Attainment Plan captures all the steps required to achieve the necessary outcomes outlined in The CEO Sales Plan.

The Sales Coach is a true coach who mentors and develops and drives a sense of urgency with both the Client Experts and The Right Team. This requires a clear understanding of where the market is going and what issues exist in the market. It also requires an innate ability to allocate the right resources at the right time to not only win Bedrock Deals, but to deliver excellent client outcomes along the way.

I'm not advocating that every Sales Coach will have all of the attributes below. This is a guide based on my own experience that helps to identify what I'd call the ideal. Broadly speaking, you will be looking for someone who has the three core competencies that form the headings in the table: Enabler, Warrior and Trainer. You might not, however, find someone who has each of these competencies to the level you require. Recruitment is often a compromise and, under these three headings, if you find one or two of these skill sets are under par, then you can train for those competencies.

Here's a table that lists the attributes of a Sales Coach:

The Sales Coach Profile		
Enabler	*Warrior*	*Trainer*
Organised	Self-aware	Patient/tolerant
Committed	Realistic	Flexible/adjustable
Process-focused	Scenario creator	Feedback-driven
Objective	Visionary	Audits strengths and weaknesses
Collaborative	Solid	
Supportive	Compassionate	Inclusive
Learning machine	Innovative	Trusting
Curious	Courageous	Balanced/fair
Awesome listener	Observant	Tough/firm
Professional	Humble	Focused
Unambiguous	Negotiator	Excellent communicator
Driven by client outcomes	Drives urgency	Constructive
Accountable		

The first competency is Enabler. The overall aspect of an Enabler is to keep the organisation out of the way to enable things to move forward. We've all heard of business prevention units. It's the Sales Coach's role to ensure the organisation understands all the issues likely to arise early enough to *enable* a planned pathway to overcome such concerns. (I'll go into more detail on this in The Power Plan section later in this book, under one of the 4C's: Control.) An Enabler is someone who doesn't feel they are indispensable to the organisation. They don't feel like they have to do everything. They are able to create, define and determine the strategy, then allow other people to execute that strategy. That's what Enablers do: they help to enable those around them to do what needs to be done.

The second competency is Warrior. A Warrior understands that within all organisations there can be roadblocks or issues that will slow that organisation down from achieving success. A Warrior is realistic enough to understand this, but also has the ability to not let these issues become too insurmountable as to derail success. They have the Warrior attitude to get things done. They will look for innovative ways around problems. They understand that there are often conflicting priorities within organisations. They can communicate this attitude to those around them, to inspire those people to think the same way as they do.

The third competency is Trainer. This is a slightly different competency in that it deals with individuals rather than the organisation as a whole. An Enabler enables the organisation to work, a Warrior drives the momentum of the organisation forward, whilst a Trainer helps those individuals in the organisation to move forward. A Trainer helps unpack issues that a Client Expert might be having with a client. They identify and help Client Experts and The Right Team develop in areas they need to. To use a sporting analogy: they are like a tennis coach working on their player's serve. They will take a video of that serve and break it down into all the various components of the action. They are able to communicate which parts of the serve are working and which parts still need work. A Trainer improves people by focusing on the detail.

In an organisation turning over $50 to $75 million, the Sales Coach would report to the CEO. In larger organisations there might be a State or Branch manager to report to, and there might be more than one Sales Coach. Client Experts report directly to the Sales Coach.

*   *   *

I've also described some of the attributes of Client Experts previously, but now I'll go into more detail. Client Experts replace traditional salespeople. In many ways the title sums up the role. Client Experts need to know their clients' businesses inside and out. They need to understand the impact on their clients at the local, regional and global level when it comes to things like a change of legislation, mergers and acquisitions of other businesses in similar industries, and emerging technological and political trends. They also need to understand the personnel within each client organisation, from the CEO down to who can help them determine their client's strategic imperatives, as well as understand within their own organisation what skills and capabilities can be brought forward to help their client meet those imperatives.

As with the Sales Coach role, I wouldn't expect every Client Expert to have all of the attributes below, but I would expect an organisation to hire someone who exhibits the vast majority of these attributes. This might sound over the top, however, I would argue that today we pay traditional IT salespeople much more than many doctors. When you consider that doctors have studied for close to a decade to become experts on the human body, and often hold the lives of their patients in their hands, then I don't think it's unreasonable for a sales organisation to want their salespeople, their Client Experts, to have a significant number of the following attributes. I believe as sales organisations, we should demand that our salespeople are experts — Client Experts.

This is a table that lists the attributes of a Client Expert:

The Client Expert Profile		
Brand Advocate	*Investigator*	*Team Player*
Confident	Adaptable, think on their feet	Teacher
Studious	Listens	Builds trust
Sociable	Disciplined	Inclusive
Professional	Persistent	Expert communicator
Time-management skills	Good judgment	Skilled storyteller
Sound reputation	Analytical	Leaves ego at the door
Driven and productive	Quick and organised thinking	Flexible
Expert market knowledge	Constructively paranoid	Balances strategy and tactics
Driven by client outcomes	Infinitely curious	Influencer
	Evidence-based behaviours	Takes initiative
		Has an attitude of abundance
		Accountable

The first competency is Brand Advocate. Client Experts are the people from the organisation whom the client sees most often. As such, Client Experts need to portray the beliefs and values of the organisation to the client with every face-to-face meeting. All those corporate and marketing capabilities that the organisation outwardly portrays on their website, or on marketing documents, and indeed to the market, must align in The Client Expert. Put simply, a client must feel and see the organisation's beliefs and values the moment your Client Expert walks through the door.

The second competency is Investigator. Whilst all three competencies are critical, this one I'd argue needs to be at least an 85% fit. An Investigator, who investigates well, is entitled to call themselves an expert. An Investigator gathers pieces of evidence and interprets this evidence. A good Investigator is able to re-interpret this evidence on the fly. They are able to pick up on nuances from a client midway through a meeting, and adapt their approach to move the deal forward. Salespeople today may meet a client with a call plan, or they may not, but often they get set in their way and aren't able to adapt to the signs that the client is giving them in a meeting to change that way. An investigator is engaged enough with the client to read those signs, and able enough to immediately adapt their pursuit of the deal in ways that accommodate those signs.

The third competency is Team Player. The bottom line here, and one of the most powerful components of The Team Plan, is that a team-based approach to selling is an infinitely better approach than that of an individual. The Client Expert will share detailed information and data with other team members and the executive of the organisation. They will help mentor and support other Client Experts. They understand completely that they are only successful because they are part of a team and, that to be more successful, they must ensure the entire team is more successful. The Remuneration Plan will help to support this understanding.

In the majority of cases, Client Experts will report to the Sales Coach. The nuance here is that if your organisation is large, then you might split the Sales Coach role into two and have a coaching role and a Client Expert leadership role. The point to make here is that every organisation is different. Under The Team Plan there will be Sales Coaches and Client Experts who will do the bulk of the selling that sales traditionally do today. There might be other members under The Team Plan devoted to transactional selling or other functions that are unique to the organisation. I acknowledge that one size won't fit all, but the principle of replacing Sales Managers with Sales Coaches and traditional salespeople with Client Experts will hold true in every case.

Here's how this new set up can look in an organisational chart:

Example Sales Structure in CEO-Led Sales

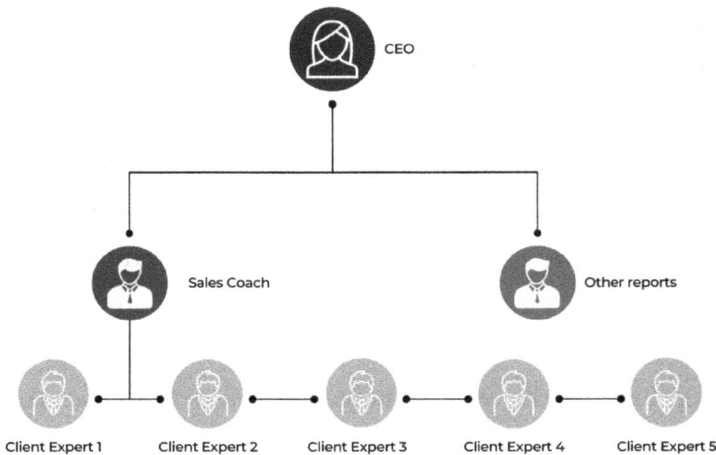

CEO

Sales Coach

Other reports

Client Expert 1   Client Expert 2   Client Expert 3   Client Expert 4   Client Expert 5

*   *   *

I've spent some time outlining the changes The Team Plan will make in sales and now I'm going to branch out from there. I've said previously that everybody who falls into the pursuit part of the organisation (and some executives from the delivery part) will be included in The Right Team. Everybody in The Right Team can be called upon by the Sales Coach and the Client Experts to drive The Deal Pursuit Plan. I've also explained earlier that the members of these Right Teams will be chosen based upon the type of client organisation and the type of deal that is being pursued. It is The Right Team for The Right Deals for The Right Clients.

For example, it's not uncommon for two Bedrock Deals to be pursued with one client. One deal could be aimed towards a structural change in the organisation, the other may relate to applications. These are two distinct areas in the client organisation. As a result, you may have some common members in each of these Right Teams or you may not. Every deal needs to be looked at on a case-by-case basis and the Team that is best placed to win the deal chosen. And anyone who isn't a Sales Coach or Client Expert could only ever participate in two deals at any one time because they have their day job to do.

I have said The Right Team would have a series of formal meetings and informal meetings, the frequency of which would depend on where the deal was in The Pursuit Plan. If the deal was four years out, then you may have a formal meeting every six months to begin with. If the deal was a couple of months out, then you might have bi-weekly meetings because the rate of change in the deal is accelerating.

Every Bedrock Deal pursuit would begin with a discovery session. Depending on the amount of information known and the length of time out from the deal, this might be anywhere from a short 30-minute catch-up to a detailed multi-hour workshop. The Sales Coach and the Client Expert would present the deal: the nuances, the facts and the assumptions.

The Pursuit Plan (which I'll cover in detail later in this book) would play an integral part of this briefing, as would The Attainment Plan that identifies The Bedrock Deal, based on The CEO Sales Plan. To use a police investigation analogy: it's as if a major crime has been committed and there's a briefing in the meeting room where everything that is known about the crime is presented and portions of work are subsequently handed out to different people.

For example, you may need to know more about a competitor, or this and that. It is the Client Expert who has the ultimate responsibility here, but they are looking to leverage all of the IP in the room to create a more complete pursuit strategy for the deal. Pieces of investigative work will be handed out to members of The Right Team to be completed across the meetings going forward.

As I've said previously, there will be informal meetings in between the formal meetings, where discoveries that either further or change these investigative pieces of work are discussed. And once again, the frequency of all meetings will increase closer to the formal process being released. This is a big change to the way deals are pursued today. I'd argue that most organisations today don't do enough research before the formal process is released. This is a fundamental problem within sales organisation today. Individual salespeople alone can't fill the gaps in their information as well as a team can.

Under The Right Model, there will still be a formal governance process over the deal and, due to the greater transparency that The Right Team brings, as opposed to an individual, this will be a lot more effective than it is today.

The only formal reporting line in The Right Team is the Client Expert to the Sales Coach. All other members of The Right Team would report to their existing line manager. For example, a legal representative in The Right Team would report to the Head of Legal. It is the members of The Right Team who hold each other accountable, whilst The Remuneration Plan, which I will explain later in this book, helps to incentivise this accountability. There is also, under The Right Team, a shift in the entire culture of the organisation from that of the individual to that of a team.

The basic premise of The Right Team is the more collaborative you can be, the more ideas you can generate and the more differing views can be brought to the table to better increase your understanding of a Bedrock Deal.

If we go back to the police investigation analogy: one person will look at a piece of evidence and probably form one conclusion. Six people will look at the same piece of evidence and may form six different conclusions. These six people may have a conversation and narrow these conclusions down to four. They will then head off and investigate each of these four conclusions thoroughly, which will result in the team learning things that the individual, who forms only one conclusion, can't.

The Right Team approach also ensures that there's more than one person focusing on the outcome, so if one of the team members has to take extended leave, then the momentum won't be lost. I've seen too many deals go away because the key player has had to take extended leave and nobody else knew what was going on.

Under The Team Plan, all employees will have the following overlay applied to their positions:

The Right Profile for all Employees			
Leadership and Ethics	*Business Acumen*	*Sales Planning and Selling*	*Technology and Solutions*
Formal leadership skills	Good planner	Competent with current tools	Understands our technology
Informal leadership skills	Understands operations	Understands the sales cycle	Understands our solutions
Good core values	Financially sound	Manages pipeline	Aware of the market
Has integrity	Marketing savvy	Understands the sales process	Aware of market issues
Always responsible	A strategic thinker	Inquiry management skills	Aware of market trends
Accountable	Focused on excellent client outcomes	Able to engage the client	
Shows Empathy	Inquisitive	Drives a Sale	
Every person hired into a CEO-led sales organisation, from the most junior to the CEO, needs to have these core skills at a competency level commensurate with their role.			

The degree of competency in each of the attributes in the table above will depend upon the role. For example, you'd expect a Client Expert and the CEO to have a high level in Technology and Solutions, whilst reception staff may only need a low to mid level. This overlay should be applied to any existing employees of the organisation as well as to any new hires.

If a level is below what is required on any of the attributes, then this can be trained. For example, you wouldn't expect a new person hired into a non-technical entry-level position to have a high level in Technology and Solutions — you would expect to train them to the right level, commensurate to their position.

One of the major benefits of The Right Profile for all Employees is that it identifies which skills need to be improved for each employee, and a constant training regime can be put in place. What ultimately underpins this overlay is the desirability of employing inquisitive people who want to learn in your organisation.

The first competency is Leadership and Ethics. Organisations today need to grow at a predictable rate and they need succession plans and a good depth of knowledge and experience. To accomplish this, organisations need people who have good leadership skills at the level required by their role. Even individual contributors, who don't have any direct reports, need leadership within themselves. They need leadership to do the right thing by the organisation and by themselves. Ethics, I think, goes without saying: no organisation wants to hire or have existing employees who don't inherently have strong personal ethics and values. I have Leadership and Ethics in the first column of the table because I believe they are fundamentals for any employee. Employees must be ethical and have the ability to lead.

The second competency is Business Acumen, which is another fundamental competency for an employee. They need to know how a commercial organisation works, what the value of delivering good outcomes is and the importance of planning. Obviously, the level of this understanding comes back to the role of the employee. For example, a CEO would need to score off the charts on this, whilst an entry-level engineer might have a middling score.

The third competency is Sales Planning and Selling. Once again, this would depend on the role in the organisation and isn't as fundamental as leadership, ethics and business acumen. As I've said previously, a junior employee with an entry-level position in the organisation might not score high on this competency, but it is something that can be trained over time. Indeed, you might find that, commensurate on the role of the employee, this is an area most employees need training on. IT organisations are pursuit organisations. They pursue deals to win deals, to then deliver deals, to then get paid to enable the pursuit of other deals. This is an infinite cycle so it's important everyone in the organisation thoroughly understands it.

The fourth competency, Technology and Solutions, is tied into this infinite cycle. To pursue and win deals and to deliver these deals successfully requires an organisation to be passionate about what they do. Whether the organisation is selling bridges, airplanes or hospitals, technology and solutions are all components of these things. Obviously, a new hire to the organisation on day one wouldn't necessarily have the depth of knowledge about the organisation, so a rigorous training program should be put in place for everyone in the organisation to explain what the organisation does, how it's done and most critically why it's done. Over time this is designed to build passion and a long-term commitment in the employee for the organisation, regardless of their level or role.

All organisations need to understand which competencies exist in their organisation and how they measure against the competency levels required for success. One platform that I can recommend to help with this measure is SEERA, the 'workforce alignment specialists' who provide online tools that enable employees to align their skills within and between organisations.

The Remuneration Plan

The Remuneration Plan is critical to support the team behaviours that underpin The Right Model. It enables an organisation to work together and understand success from a client and solution perspective, and to continually plan, execute, review, learn and update. The Remuneration Plan applies to Sales Coaches, Client Experts and the members of The Right Team who are pursuing a deal.

There are five key components in the structure of The Remuneration Plan:

Remuneration Plan Components

1. Base Salary

The first is the base salary which, as we know, is the salary an individual is paid to do their job. The difference in The Remuneration Plan from what occurs today is that the base salary paid to Client Experts will be below the current industry average, because of the importance of the second component of The Remuneration Plan (The Right Contribution). I'd recommend this to be approximately 80% of the current level, but this would vary depending on the level of maturity in the market and the type of resource you're going after. This might sound like a hard sell when hiring the talent required, but there are some important differences in The Remuneration Plan to what happens today.

The first is that through The Right Contribution employees have the potential to be paid above the industry average base salary, if they successfully exhibit The Right Behaviours. The second is that salaries are not tied to a 12-month cycle, they are tied to success. The third is that The Right Model creates an organisation which is a better place to work, where the support and guidance of team structures that are remunerated on team success will attract people who are looking for rewarding long-term employment in a team culture. I will go into more detail on each of these three things in this section.

I'd recommend the Sales Coach be paid 120% of the current industry average. This is to recognise the importance of leadership in The Right Model attracting the best talent to this position. All other members of The Right Team will be paid 100% of their base salary because the organisation needs to attract the best talent to do their day jobs. The bonus structure will shift away from the current metrics, tied to the technical aspects of their roles today, towards team-based bonuses, which I will soon explain.

2. The Right Contribution

The second component of The Remuneration Plan is The Right Contribution:

The Right Contribution

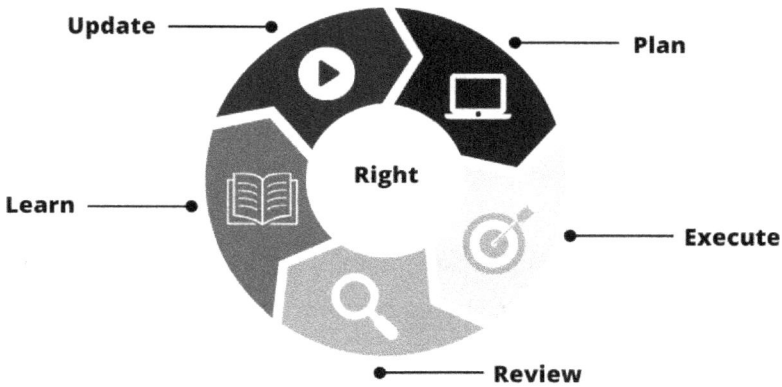

The Right Contribution is different to how most remuneration is handled today and critically important to The Right Model. I have said previously how important it is to understand your client's strategic imperatives and the direction they're headed in, alongside being globally, locally and regionally aware to understand how change will affect the client. The better informed you are about these things, the better you can plan and execute to improve your ability to win Bedrock Deals. This continuum of plan, execute, review, learn and update is critically important to The Right Model. It is the foundation of The Right Model, so it needs to be measured and incentivised separately.

The Right Contribution isn't a sit-down-and-tick-the-box-with-your-manager-to-get-paid exercise, as so many KPI (Key Performance

Indicator) mechanisms currently are today. Success here has to be agreed to by all the contributing members in the deal pursuit: the Client Expert, the Sales Coach and the members of The Right Team. It needs to be a transparent and a mature process. All parties must agree that the deal is moving forward because The Right Model is being successfully applied. I can't over-emphasise the importance of The Right Contribution. This is the contribution that sets up every other portion of The Remuneration Plan and ultimately delivers the true CEO-led sales organisation.

The Right Contribution review would be tied to the cycle of reviews that occurs around the Pursuit, Attainment and CEO Sales Plans. For example, if The Bedrock Deal was four years out, that review might be every six months; if The Bedrock Deal was, say, six months out, that review might be weekly. No matter how often the review is undertaken, the essence here is the deal must have momentum. There are only two reasons why a deal wouldn't have momentum.

The first is the client's priorities have changed because there's an external factor that has changed, over which you've got no control, and couldn't see coming. For example, a change in legislation or government policy. I was once involved in a $20 million deal with a large government agency working with social services. We'd been notified of our success on the Friday, but, over the following weekend, the Prime Minister announced a change in policy that reallocated funding away from the deal we'd just won.

The second reason is that the Client Expert or The Right Team haven't pushed it forward. In the latter case, obviously The Right Contribution wouldn't be paid.

I'd recommend The Right Contribution be paid every six months because this is long enough to measure behaviour and short enough to be motivational. The Contribution would reset every six-month period (i.e. each period is self-contained).

I'd also recommend the payment be 40% of the base salary for Client Experts. So, effectively, if you are a Client Expert who is performing consistently well, this equates to 112% of the current industry average base salary (80% + (40% of 80% = 32%) = 112%). I'd recommend a Sales Coach be paid 20% of their base salary, which recognises that they are already being paid 20% above the industry average.

Other members of The Right Team will be paid 10% of their base, if they receive The Right Contribution, which roughly brings them in line with the Client Experts, i.e. if they display The Right Behaviours, they will receive 110% of their base salary.

If a Team member misses The Right Contribution, then there is clearly a performance issue that needs to be uncovered. Whilst The Team Plan builds a culture of accountability, it is team-based accountability, so there needs to be clear communication within the team around why one member mightn't be meeting their goals. This is a culture of empathy alongside performance.

This might sound like a contradiction, but The Right Contribution can still be paid even if there's no momentum in a deal. As I said previously, there are two reasons for a deal not to have momentum. If it's due to the lack of performance of the team, then the contribution wouldn't be paid. If it's due to an external factor outside of The Right Team's control, then as long as all the planning, execution, review, learning and updating was up to date, then the Right Contribution would be paid.

This contribution is based upon successful Right behaviours, not fiscal outcomes. Underpinning this is that successful behaviours under The Right Model lead to winning deals. And I know I've said this previously, but to identify this lack of momentum as early as possible in the deal life cycle is critical. There are only so many resources an organisation has, and to keep chasing deals that are dead is a waste for everyone concerned. To be able to identify dead deals early and devote resources away from these deals is success in itself, and the team responsible for uncovering this deserves to receive The Right Contribution. Regardless of how The Right Contribution is set up, strong leadership needs to be in place. It is strong leadership that drives and ensures the Right Behaviours long term.

3. The Success Contribution

The third component of The Remuneration Plan is The Success Contribution. The Success Contribution helps turn the organisation to face the client because the majority of the organisation's targets are set on the clients, not the individuals. I say 'the majority' because this needs to be uniquely applied to each organisation depending on what market it operates in and the type of things it is selling.

Ideally, the bigger The Bedrock Deal, the higher the quota placed on the client. The inverse is also true. For example, you might have your Right Team pursuing a $40 million Bedrock Deal. The Client Expert on that deal would likely have 95% of their quota placed on the client and 5% placed on them individually. This ensures a team-based approach to deliver the best outcomes for the client. At the other end of the scale, you might have a junior Client Expert pursuing a Stepping Stone deal with a client. In this case, they might have 80% of their quota placed on the client and 20% placed upon them individually. It all depends on what needs to be rewarded and under what circumstances.

Every Client would have a Success Contribution applied to it. Every member of The Right Team would have the opportunity to be paid The Success Contribution. As a Client Expert, you would have a number of Bedrock Deals that are closing over multiple yearly time frames, with potentially more than one Bedrock Deal with one client. There is complexity here and this would be captured in a 3D-style layout. Having said this, The Success Contribution to be paid in the next 12 months would be very clear, as it would apply to those Bedrock Deals that are about to close. The Success Contribution is paid monthly and is contingent upon The Right Contribution being earned in the same period.

I'd recommend The Success Contribution be paid to Client Experts at 40% of base salary with 70% achievement required. This total of 40% would only be paid if 100% of the quota was reached, and would be paid pro-rata as long as 70% achievement was met.

For example, if 90% of the quota was reached, 36% (90% of 40%) of the base salary would be paid. Over-achievement would be capped at 25%. For example, if there was a quota of $20 million on a client and The Bedrock Deal delivered $60 million, then a maximum of 25% over-achievement would be paid, not 300%. The additional over-achievement is capped at 50% and then paid into the Pool and Evolve Components.

I'd also recommend the Success Component be paid slightly less to the Sales Coach at 30% of base, and 10% to the other members of The Right Team. I'm not advocating this is the only way to apply The Success Contribution; all of these percentages could and should be tailored to each organisation.

The CEO, the CFO, the Sales Coach, or your governance model would set the Success Component sales quotas for the year. These quotas would be based on the figures the board or your governance body has set for the financial year. For example, a 10% growth quota on the previous year might have been set, so that would form the numbers for that year. As I've said previously, this short-term approach is a problem with how numbers are set today. The reality here is this is the way the business world works.

Under The Right Model, however, there will be more transparency and confidence around these annual numbers. For example, The CEO Sales Plan might determine that the organisation should move into security-managed services over the next four years. The Sales Coach and Client Experts have developed a strategy in The Attainment Plan for this to occur. The Sales Coach, CEO, CFO or the governance body would sit down at the three- or four-year point, knowing the security managed-services Bedrock Deals that are left in the pipeline are the ones on track according to The Pursuit Plan that has been constantly tested by The Power Plan (which I'll explain in the next sections). The quotas put against these clients would reflect this rigour, and the confidence of landing these deals would therefore be high.

The CEO would be backing the board's growth number because they know the deals can be won and why. The Right Team would also be confident they can achieve their quotas and get paid The Success Contribution because they have received The Right Contribution over a number of years for these deals, i.e. they have exhibited the right long-term behaviours around planning, execution, review, learning and updating. The Success Contribution rewards The Right Team around the annual fiscal quotas, whilst The Right Contribution ensures those Bedrock Deals further out are being managed. This intersection is where the necessary annual success of the organisation and the long-term, infinite cycle of business is considered and accommodated.

There is little doubt implementing The Success Contribution on day one of The Right Model would require care and attention to avoid the pitfalls of rewarding individual behaviours that are not consistent with the CEO Sales Plan. This is one of the reasons why the Sales Coach's remuneration structure is different to the Client Expert's, because long-term vision and strategic leadership need to be instilled on day one. Over time, as transparency within the short- and long-term pipe-line is revealed, accountability within the teams is created, and all the other benefits of The Right Model are realised, the risk of rewarding apparent or actual inconsistencies will diminish. I think it's important to note that the value of The Success Contribution is something that will improve as the momentum of The Right Model picks up.

4. The Pool Contribution

The fourth component of The Remuneration Plan is The Pool Contribution. The Pool Contribution, like the overall Remuneration Plan, is intended to move the organisation to face the client, to build team behaviours, and to encourage employees to think strategically in relation to understanding client and organisational goals. The Pool Contribution allows the Sales Coach, the Client Expert and The Right Team to receive a bonus, even if it hasn't sold or been involved in a Bedrock Deal over the assigned period, which is 12 months. This recognises that the key to exceptional leadership is taking responsibility by driving and leading The Right Behaviours.

There are a number of metrics that need to be met in order to pay The Pool Contribution, such as: The Right Contribution has been met over the 12-month period, and the overall organisation has achieved its number for that same period. The Success Contribution doesn't need to be achieved.

For example, you might be a Client Expert and you've exhibited all of The Right Behaviours over the last 12 months to receive The Right Contribution, but along the way you have determined, by applying the Power Plan, that the organisation is better off devoting their resources to pursuing other Bedrock Deals than your own. The Pool Contribution ensures that you are still able to receive a bonus for the year, even though you missed The Success Contribution. Indeed, The Pool Contribution will encourage you to support your colleagues whose Bedrock Deals are still alive, so they can be won and the organisation can make the number for the year and The Pool Contribution can be paid. The Pool Contribution helps to build an organisation that is united and focused on organisational success, not individual success.

As I said previously, the funds in The Pool Contribution come from over-achievement in The Success Contribution. I'd recommend The Pool Contribution be 10% of the base salary for a Client Expert and 5%

for the Sales Coach and the other members of The Right Team. This would either be paid or not be paid, i.e. a Client Expert would either receive The Pool Contribution at 10% or receive nothing. The Pool Contribution is paid annually.

In addition to receiving The Right Contribution and the organisation making the number for the year, there are a number of other metrics that need to be put in place for The Pool Contribution to be paid. These metrics will be clearly defined by The CEO of the organisation well prior to the 12-month period they cover. The CEO determines who gets paid what, based upon the metrics they have set. These metrics need to be objective so everyone in The Right Team knows exactly what needs to happen for them to receive The Pool Contribution.

I make this point because the philosophy here needs to be simplicity and clarity. I have worked in organisations where there are so many metrics set to achieve a bonus that it is nearly impossible to receive that payment. An overly complex or opaque system discourages employees, because they usually give up when they realise they've missed one very small metric, or they just inherently know the system is set up in a way that the likelihood of them receiving the payment is close to zero, even when the organisation overall has made its number for the year.

The Pool Contribution metrics will cover five key areas: The CEO Sales Plan, Company, Individual, Client Experience/Outcome, and Team Player/Culture. The number of metrics covering each area will be minimal and should essentially be the most important metrics for the organisation.

An example of The CEO Sales Plan metric is simply that The Right Clients and The Right Deals, as defined by the plan, are being pursued.

An example of a Company metric could be profit margin, such as the organisation will deliver a 21% profit margin for the year. It could also be the overall revenue number, as I have mentioned.

An example of an Individual metric, which I have also mentioned, is that you have received your Right Contribution over the period.

An example of a Client Experience/Outcome metric could be a certain Net Promoter Score. The Net Promoter Score is a worthwhile process, however, I think there are some problems with how it is applied today. The first problem is that it isn't applied broadly enough, usually only to certain sized engagements and clients. The second problem is that it's usually applied by the sales team, who tend to manipulate the outcomes because their remuneration is based upon it. (Remember the research from Bain & Company that I've previously mentioned, where 80% of CEOs believe they deliver a superior customer experience whilst only 8% of their clients agree.) Salespeople today do this by nominating the individuals within the client organisation that they know will give them a good score.

If, however, the Net Promoter Score is applied randomly and broadly within the client, independent from The Right Team involved with the client, and if it is regularly applied (more than once a year), then I believe it is a good objective metric for Client Experience/Outcome.

Otherwise, the Net Promoter Score needs to either be applied differently, or another measure needs to be put into place. One that is simple, broad-based and open to fluctuations. Like an app-based approach where people can register and there's a measure in there to determine that users are answering the questions truly, i.e. not just giving every question the same score. If this can occur, then the score for Client Experience/Outcome will be objective.

An example of a Team Player/Culture metric that is utterly objective is more challenging to discern. Whilst the first three areas can have clearly defined numbers placed on them, Team Player/Culture is more of a feeling. How well did someone participate as a team member to make the entire organisation successful? This is a little grey, but I'd argue that it's a really easy thing to see in a team-based culture. You are either part of the team or you are not. There may need to be a number of inputs across the organisation to measure this, but I reckon it would be fairly clear.

5. The Evolve Contribution

The fifth component of The Remuneration Plan is The Evolve Contribution. The Evolve Contribution drives a long-term mindset in the organisation, especially in the Sales Coach and Client Expert roles. This area of the organisation today, the sales area, typically has a high turnover of staff, as detailed in the 2018 Bridge Group report[4] where the average sales rep tenure is now 1.5 years, down from 3 years in 2010. The Evolve Contribution addresses this turnover. It also rewards sustained excellence and longevity outside of winning additional business, which encourages your best staff to stay in your organisation long term.

---

4   https://blog.bridgegroupinc.com/2018-sdr-metrics-report

The Evolve Contribution is funded by over-achievement in The Success Contribution and covers the period outlined by The CEO Sales Plan. For example, if the CEO Sales Plan covers the next four years, then The Evolve Contribution would be paid at the end of that four-year period. Given The CEO Sales Plan evolves each year to reflect the changes in the market and the client base, so essentially every year there is an updated four-year CEO Sales Plan. The Evolve Contribution would therefore apply to The CEO Sales Plan annually, so it would become an incentive offered each year.

The Evolve Contribution metrics cover the same five key areas that The Pool Contribution covers: The CEO Sales Plan, Company, Individual, Client Experience/Outcome, and Team Player/Culture. Whilst the measures in The Pool Contribution are predominately quantitative, the Evolve Contribution metrics are qualitative.

The Pool Contribution metrics would form the basis for 80-90% of the Evolve Contribution metrics. As qualitative metrics, these will be more subjective and harder to determine than The Pool Contribution quantitative metrics, but they should still be built on defined outcomes.

For example, the Company metric in The Pool Contribution might be to achieve the number for the year at a defined profit level. The Evolve Contribution will take these metrics and extrapolate them further, delivering a metric of something like: are we now the market leader in our segment of the market? This metric combines the Company metric, of profit and revenue, with the Client Experience/Outcome metric: are we delivering excellent client experiences? The determination here would be whether or not an industry analyst firm has recognised our organisation as having a 'top-right quadrant' solution in our area of the market. If the answer is 'yes', then those metrics must be judged to be successfully met.

As with The Pool Contribution, these metrics will be determined by the CEO and be clearly communicated to the Sales Coach, the Client Experts and The Right Team each year. Unlike The Pool Contribution, where you might have a different metric for different individuals, the metrics for the Evolve Contribution will be the same for everyone, aligning the qualitative goals of the organisation.

The Right Contribution, at least an average 70% of The Success Contribution, and The Pool Contribution must be achieved each year of The CEO Sales Plan that the Evolve Contribution covers for the Evolve Contribution to be paid. I'd recommend these payments be 20% of the base salary for the Sales Coach and the Clients Experts, and 10% for other members in The Right Team. It is paid as a lump sum at the end of The CEO Sales Plan period.

For example, if I were a Client Expert and I achieved the Evolve Contribution, and the CEO Sales Plan covered a four-year period, then I would be paid up to (20% x 4 =) 80% of my base salary that year. I say 'up to', because obviously the funds need to be in the Evolve Pool for the entire 80% to be paid as this is funded completely by the over-achievement in The Success Contribution, so it doesn't cost the organisation anything extra.

The premise here is to take those huge bonuses paid to traditional salespeople for landing a huge deal, reduce that payment in The Success Contribution, placing a portion of what is left over in The Pool

Contribution to drive The Right Behaviours, while the Evolve Contribution encourages and rewards longevity and sustained excellence.

10. The Right Deals

THE RIGHT MODEL

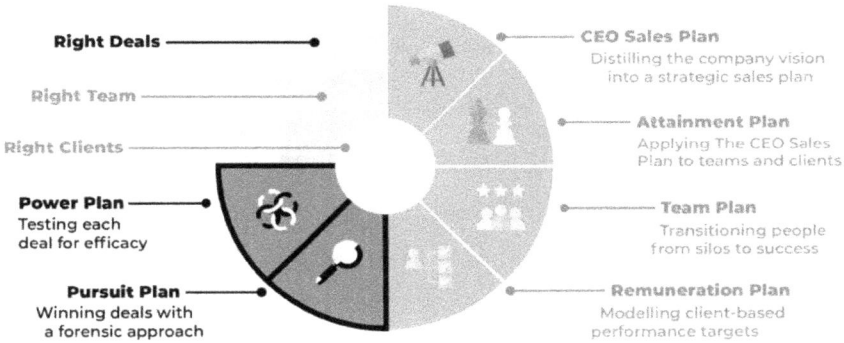

Right Deals

Right Team

Right Clients

Power Plan
Testing each
deal for efficacy

Pursuit Plan
Winning deals with
a forensic approach

CEO Sales Plan
Distilling the company vision
into a strategic sales plan

Attainment Plan
Applying The CEO Sales
Plan to teams and clients

Team Plan
Transitioning people
from silos to success

Remuneration Plan
Modelling client-based
performance targets

The Right Deals are multi-solution Bedrock Deals. They align the clients and the solutions The CEO Sales Plan and The Attainment Plan have identified. They also align all the resources and key competencies of the organisation, or the team, with the strategy for the future that the CEO has outlined in The CEO Sales Plan. The Right Deals lead the organisation towards success.

For example, The Attainment Plan will have outlined the invested solutions for Bedrock Deals that need to be pursued over a matrix period of time:

INVESTED SOLUTIONS FOR
BEDROCK DEALS MATRIX

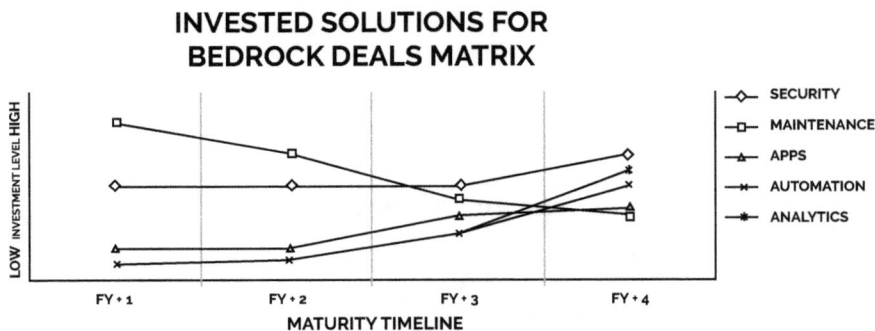

The Invested Solutions for Bedrock Deals Matrix outlines the solutions that will mature over, say, the next 12 to 18 months. It will develop another set of solutions to come in at that 18-month mark, which will be in place until, say, the four-year mark. And at that four-year mark, The CEO Sales Plan will outline the next steps.

In this example, The Right Deals are the deals that contain one or more of those solutions. You may have a Right Deal at the three-year mark that uses three solutions within that matrix which The CEO Sales Plan has outlined. A Right Deal is more powerful when it has more than one solution, because the more solutions that can be delivered, the easier it becomes to build a unique sales proposition with the client. As we know, the more unique you can make your offering, the more likely it is to increase your value with the client, and the more likely they will be willing to pay for your offering.

It also enables you to bring in the right partners on the deal. You will be able to partner for capability, not convenience, which is important. Over the years, I've seen salespeople bring in a partner many times purely because it is convenient. That partner may already have an existing relationship with the client, or that partner might have excess resources that they offer at a cheap price. It is always capability, not convenience, that delivers true value for the client.

Having said that, there might be an occasion when you win a deal that isn't a Right Deal, but it keeps your competitors away from your client. In this situation, finding a partner who can deliver that deal better than you should be adopted. Delivering a deal poorly because it doesn't align with your organisation's resources and key competencies will damage your prospects for future business with that client.

The Pursuit Plan

The Pursuit Plan identifies and details The Right Deals: The Bedrock Deal and all the Stepping Stone Deals that lead up to that Bedrock Deal. Every Bedrock Deal has a unique Pursuit Plan. It is created and owned by the Client Expert, with coaching and guidance from the Sales Coach and The Right Team. Whilst The CEO Sales Plan might have a creative input of 80% CEO and 20% IP owners, and The Attainment Plan might have a creative input of roughly 50% Client Expert and 50% Sales Coach, The Pursuit Plan is more likely to be 80% Client Expert and 20% Sales Coach and Right Team.

The Pursuit Plan covers the time period of the deal it describes. For example, one Pursuit Plan might cover the renewal of a contract with a client over an 18-month period. This plan would contain a combination of activities to convince the client to renew beforehand, i.e. stop the tender going to market, alongside building uniqueness with that client, so if the deal did go to tender, then the organisation would be in a good position to win it.

On the other hand, you might have a Pursuit Plan based on The CEO Sales Plan that wants the organisation to get into transport in the future. The organisation at that point might not have any transport clients. The Client Expert and the Sales Coach might identify a major transport and logistics company as the client with the attributes the CEO has described. It might require a five-year Pursuit Plan to influence this major transport and logistics company through conversations and Stepping Stone Deals to eventually win that Right Deal.

The Pursuit Plans are the organisation's Bedrock Deal bibles. They document the agreed success strategy for the pursuit of these Bedrock Deals. They are central to the Client Expert role. Client Experts would refer to some Pursuit Plans daily, and others less so, depending on where the deal was in its life cycle. For example, if the deal was going to close in a couple of months, the plan might be referred to daily. If the deal was going to close in five years' time, then less so, maybe once every fortnight.

This might sound like overkill, but, for example, you might have a client event next week that details a security offering. And you might also want that client you're targeting five years out with a security offering to attend that same event and sit next to one of your clients to whom you are currently delivering a security offering. That's the power of Pursuit Plans: they structure the long term into steps that a Client Expert needs to take in the lead-up to a future deal that will greatly improve the likelihood of winning that deal. It also fully documents the success strategy for the organisation which minimises the impact of any staff changes.

The Pursuit Plan contains three core parts:

1. The Client

This describes the client in detail. It looks at such things as their annual turnover, their industry, their major competitors and customers, their business structure, number of staff and offices, and so on. It describes how and why the client aligns to both The CEO Sales Plan and The Attainment Plan. It interrogates how the client thinks, what their core beliefs are: their mission, their rallying cause, their vision.

It also clearly outlines the strategic imperatives of the client. It asks: What has been said in the press by that client about what they want to achieve, and over what time frame? And how, as an organisation, do we fit into that future?

It is crucial to understand these imperatives and how your organisation fits with them, so a significant amount of time may be required. You might spend a year visiting a client to build this knowledge. It is important because it will help you to frame your future conversations with the client. It will also help you to identify the right people in the organisation to have these conversations with. This will enable you to see those deals coming up in their future that perhaps the client hasn't seen for themselves. If you don't understand your client's strategic imperatives, then at best you're responding to what everyone else is doing in the market, and at worst you're effectively stabbing in the dark.

For example, your client might be a bank and the CEO has said in the press that they want to open offices throughout Asia. This is their strategic imperative. To achieve this imperative you might identify 50 business problems the client needs to solve. Of these problems, 10 might relate to the solutions your organisation can deliver. Knowing this strategic imperative helps you to understand the importance of your solutions to the client. Essentially, it enables you to speak the same language as the client.

For example, you might have a useful reference site: 'It's really interesting you're wanting to open offices in Thailand. We've just helped a client in the US do the same thing, and here are some of the issues we discovered ...' Speaking the same language as the client places you in a very strong position to be able to influence them towards your solutions.

2. The Team

This lists the team members from the organisation working on the deal. It lists the mechanical team, i.e. the bid manager, the bid editors and the pricing analysts. It also lists The Right Team, which I have explained in the previous section as the team that would include the Client Expert, the Sales Coach and four other members from the organisation who bring the best possible skills and experience to the team relevant to the deal.

A big distinction I'd like to make here between these two teams is that one simply gets deals through the internal systems (Mechanical) whilst the other is qualitatively reviewing and creating the deal strategy (Right Team). I make this distinction because today the mechanical team often have far too much influence in the strategy of the deal.

Many times I've seen situations where the strategy for a deal has changed because the bid manager decided that the organisation didn't have the resources to chase that solution, or the approved margin has arbitrarily been put up to 21% and the deal is currently running at 18%, as well as a variety of other reasons. And I've seen examples where these strategy changes aren't discovered by the team until after the deal has been lost. I'm not advocating that deal governance shouldn't be adhered to, what I'm saying is deal governance needs to be viewed holistically across the deal, not tactically. The Pursuit Plan ensures the best-equipped people, or the brains trust, will ultimately deliver the optimum deal strategy.

3. The Deal

This describes the deal in detail under three headings:

a. Background

This articulates what the deal is and how it supports The CEO Sales Plan. Specifically, it lists the practical details of the deal such as the expected release date, the expected submission date, the incumbent, the role of the organisation in the deal, the solutions the deal is pursuing, and what outcomes those solutions will deliver for the client. It describes how all these details link back to the organisational strategy contained in The CEO Sales Plan.

This is a big difference from how things are done today. Typically today an organisation will pursue a deal that the client has created, i.e. responding to an existing client need. In The Right Model Pursuit

Plan, the organisation is pursuing a deal that the organisation has primarily created, i.e. identifying and developing a need for the client.

The role of the organisation in the practical details refers to such things as whether the organisation is part of a consortium. It will describe who the partners are and outline what significant value you're leveraging from them. It will describe whether your organisation is leading the consortium or whether your organisation is an individual. A description of the incumbent will include what that competitor is doing in the marketplace today. Not only in terms of the industry the deal relates to, but in what other relevant industry verticals the incumbent is doing business.

This is really important because it will help you to understand your second-most important competitor. I say 'second-most' because your most important competitor is the client doing nothing. Doing nothing would be resigning themselves to the incumbent. This could happen not because the incumbent is doing a good job, but because we, as the alternative, didn't do a good enough job in creating the need in the client to change.

The same is true if you are the incumbent. If, as the incumbent, you are simply delivering the requirements perfectly, then you risk a competitor coming in with a significant point of difference that convinces the client to change. In this case, as the incumbent, you haven't done enough to self-disrupt, which is your competitor's approach. If you don't self-disrupt, then you run the risk that if your client is convinced to change by your competitors, you will lose out.

You might find some of these details will be blank, for example, the expected release date. If you are creating a deal that will close in some years' time, then that date won't be fully realised.

For example, I will use the scenario of the major transport and logistics company that I mentioned earlier. The CEO has identified that the future of the organisation lies in transport. The Sales Coach and Client Expert have identified an opportunity with the major transport and logistics company coming up in five years' time, or the organisation has a solution that is being developed that is going to mature in five years' time. The Client Expert might have only just started work on creating the need in the major transport and logistics company, so obviously the timing of the intersection of either the deal coming to market or the solution being mature isn't fully clear yet. In this case, it's fine not to have an expected release date — that will arrive closer to time. The important part is to understand why it's an important deal to pursue.

b. Ecosystem

This describes three things: your Right Team, your Partners and your Competitors.

This puts the team into the context of the deal. It outlines the strengths and the weaknesses of the team and formulates the best strategy or approach for the client. It also puts your partners into the context of the deal. It determines what exactly each partner brings to the table and formulates the best approach to bringing your partners into the deal process. It also describes who your competitors might be.

I don't believe you need to go into a huge amount of detail about your competitors. You might find if you're pursuing a deal from a long way out that your organisation is the only one pursuing that deal. In this case, you would speculate on who the competitors might be. As you get closer to the deal, you might be able to identify the competitors more meaningfully, but, in this case, if you have been pursuing the deal from a long way out, then your competitors are playing catch-up.

If there is an incumbent, then that is your most worthy competitor and you must be able to present your organisation as a worthy alternative to the incumbent. You must also differentiate your offer enough to give the client a reason to choose your organisation over the incumbent. And if you are the incumbent, you've got to self-disrupt to give the client a reason to keep you and ensure the value of the deal either increases or is maintained, i.e. there's reduced downward pressure on price due to efficiency dividends.

c.   Financials and Commercials

This covers the value and term of the deal, as well as the estimated date the contract will be signed. Once again, if you're chasing a deal from a long way off, these financials won't be as clear as if the deal was closing in, say, nine months' time when they should be very clear. If they are not clear nine months out, then, as a CEO, alarms bells should be going off because that indicates the team don't know enough about the deal, which surely signifies that your chances of winning that deal are very slim indeed.

*   *   *

The final detail about the deal that is captured in The Pursuit Plan is the VantagePoint. This brings together the culture of the client you are pursuing, your own culture, and the unique value you are bringing to that client into a 'we believe' statement. This statement is very challenging to develop, but is very, very powerful when you are meeting with your client's senior executives, because this will differentiate you from your competitors without talking about technology or business problems or strategic imperatives. Your VantagePoint will encapsulate all of these things in an emotive and passionate statement.

Using my earlier example of a public sector opportunity with a state government that dealt with family services, we created a VantagePoint something like: 'We believe all children have the right to live in a safe, healthy, respectful environment that nurtures and develops them.'

We specifically outlined to the client all the things we had done as an organisation that align to this VantagePoint. This was a verbal description of a strategic imperative blended with the solution we were offering, based upon the culture of both organisations. This was incredibly powerful because it not only motivated the team, but it let the client know what we stood for. It differentiated us from the competition because we weren't regurgitating the strategic imperative. We weren't saying what everyone else was saying: 'I read in your annual report that you want to reduce child abuse by 30% in the next 12 months.' We were saying something different that aligned our team to the client.

Ideally, The Pursuit Plan and the analytics measuring the effectiveness of the plan should all be built into the CRM. It is the Client Expert's responsibility to ensure the CRM is up to date every week.

This will not only enable the organisation to get real-time reporting, but ensure the organisation stays on track with each deal. It will also enable the CEO to have absolute transparency on the organisation's current state of play for each deal.

Ultimately, The Pursuit Plan enables an organisation to monitor and manage Bedrock Deals over whatever time frame necessary. It also ensures the deals fit with the future direction of the organisation. It also creates a powerful ecosystem of Stepping Stone Deals that lead up to The Bedrock Deal. This is important because it focuses the organisation on the deals that are the most important to win.

Using the major transport and logistics company example once more, the in-five-years'-time Bedrock Deal might be to redevelop their HR system. To win this deal, The Pursuit Plan will tell us that we have to prove our credibility in consulting with them. It will outline that one Stepping Stone deal will be to sell them a small consultation to review their cloud strategy. This deal is seemingly unrelated to The Bedrock Deal, but we know through The Pursuit Plan that eventually The Bedrock Deal is going to have to run in the cloud.

If we lose that deal, say, to the incumbent, then the next Stepping Stone deal might be around their licensing arrangements. Once again, this might not be related to The Bedrock Deal, but because we lost the consulting deal to the incumbent, we must change our strategy. We can decide to discount the deal to a level that's irresistible. If we don't win that deal, then obviously the client is telling us to go away, which is a good message to receive early on.

If we do win the deal while not making our desired margins, it enables us to have a foothold to begin to build credibility with them as part of our long-term strategy. I have to make the point here that I'm not advocating discounting a deal to a loss-making level, nor discounting a deal that doesn't have a clear linkage to the overall strategy for that client. I'd suggest in this example that you'd need to win more than one Stepping Stone Deal to be able to prove the credibility required to win The Bedrock Deal.

The major transport and logistics company will be highly unlikely to trust an organisation they haven't done significant business with before with the redevelopment of their HR system. And, alternatively, if our organisation hasn't done significant business with the major transport and logistics company before, then it's unlikely we know their business well enough to be able to convince them we are the best organisation to do so. Unless we heavily discount the deal, which as I've explained previously, becomes a lose-lose. The major transport and logistics company receive a poorly resourced job, whilst our organisation likely loses money on the deal.

The ecosystem of Stepping Stone Deals leading up to winning a Bedrock Deal is one of the most powerful elements of The Pursuit Plan. It delivers a long-term, transparent and detailed deal strategy fully aligned to the long-term strategic direction the CEO has set for the organisation.

The Power Plan

The Power Plan overlays The Pursuit Plan. It tests the efficacy of a Bedrock Deal. It reviews the deal through the lens of the four critical components: Credibility, Capability, Commitment and Control. What I call the 4C's:

Power Plan

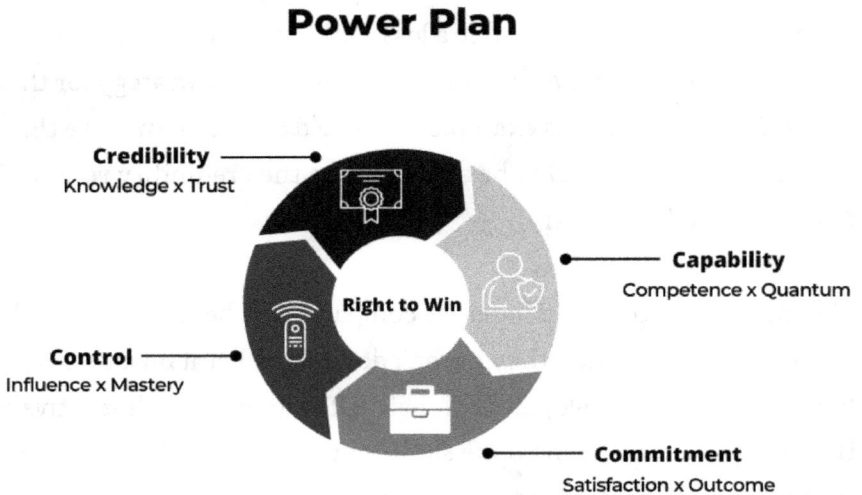

The Power Plan establishes a rating system out of 100 for each of the 4C's where 100 is the highest right-to-win rating for a Bedrock Deal. Component scores are then combined to deliver an overall rating out of 100. Each component is critical and must be present, measuring at least 60 for you to have a high right-to-win rating. For example, if you measured 100 across three of these components but 0 for the fourth, then your right-to-win rating would probably come out at an overall score of less than 50. The combined or overall score needs to be 80 or more for an organisation to have a high right-to-win rating. A high right-to-win rating means the organisation is well positioned to win The Bedrock Deal.

I use the term 'right to win' because I've seen some deals that measured 0 under my system that were still won. All of these deals were compromised in some way in terms of delivery, margin or people and so on. The right to win refers to landing The Bedrock Deal on your own terms with a good margin, and good delivery and so on. The right to win refers to winning The Right Deals.

I will be using this term throughout this section. The Power Plan is a snapshot of a moment in time during the life of the deal that can be applied at any point to measure whether the deal is on track. It can stand alone as an independent diagnostic tool to measure the efficacy of a deal, regardless of what sales methodology is in place.

Below is an example of a Power Plan score. I will be going into the detail of how these scores are derived in this section.

Power Plan Score

4C's	Factors	Factors	Total
	Knowledge	Trust	
Credibility	8	10	80
	Competence	Quantum	
Capability	7	9	63
	Satisfaction	Outcome	
Commitment	9	8	72
	Influence	Mastery	
Control	10	9	90
		Total	305
		Right to Win	**76.25/100**

The Power Plan is primarily applied to Bedrock Deals — those long-term deals identified in The CEO Sales Plan that transform both the client and the organisation. Using the earlier major transport and logistics company example, you might find that in the beginning of that pursuit there is an opportunity arising in five years' time that you begin with a 0 in all four components. That's absolutely fine. The Power Plan will direct the Client Expert, the Sales Coach and The

Right Team on the important aspects they need to build over time to improve the rating in each of those four components.

It also guides the ecosystem of Stepping Stone Deals that need to be won with the client to improve the rating in some of those components. It also enables the CEO at any moment in that five-year period leading up to the deal to quickly and easily measure the effectiveness of the Client Expert, the Sales Coach and The Right Team in their pursuit of the deal.

Each component within The Power Plan has a benchmark question where the majority of the rating is usually assigned with sub-questions beneath, which add smaller weights. The importance in the rating of the benchmark questions allows The Power Plan to be applied quickly and easily if need be, simply by answering four questions. The answers and ratings are subjective because they require the client, the deal, the team and the organisation, relative to the timeline of the deal, to be contextualised. This will become clearer when we talk through each of the four components.

Like The Pursuit Plan, The Power Plan view would be applied less often when the deal was, say, five years out, than if it was one year out. For example, it might be applied quarterly when five years out, then weekly one year out. The Power Plan is applied by the CEO with input from the Client Expert, The Right Team and the Sales Coach. Once applied at a moment in time, it generates a number of key outcomes that then flow back into The Pursuit Plan as action points for the Client Expert, The Right Team and the Sales Coach to follow up. The Power Plan enables deals to be measured throughout their life cycle against each other.

I've spoken about putting all deals into the pipeline, then qualifying them out over time. For example, you might have four deals in the pipeline at one time that have all arrived in their cycle where they need significant resources devoted to them (you wouldn't qualify a deal out before this juncture as they aren't yet demanding a high level of resourcing). You might only have enough resources to cover two of those deals. The Power Plan allows you to objectively make the decision of which two deals are best to pursue and which two you need to walk away from.

In this case, The Power Plan might determine that three out of the four deals are fundamental to the success of the organisation, as defined in The CEO Sales Plan. It might also determine that the organisation has a high likelihood of winning each of those three deals. In this case, you might then decide to bring more resources in, to look at partners, or hiring in more capability.

This is one of the most powerful aspects of The Power Plan. It delivers a measure that enables an organisation to make well-informed strategic decisions about the best deals to pursue that will lead to long-term success for the organisation.

It also delivers absolute transparency to the Client Expert and The Right Team as to why the pursuit of one deal was chosen over another, which in itself also helps to create a clear road map for what needs to be done in future deals to get them over the line. This also promotes organisational success over individual success, which goes a long way to creating a positive and driven team-based organisational culture.

The Power Plan represents a big change from the way deals are assessed today. There are many deal methodologies out there, and the majority of them are a step-by-step process from the bottom up, examining whether the salesperson has a good relationship with technical and legal and HR and marketing and so on. Tick, tick, tick, tick.

These things are important to have, but of themselves they won't necessarily change the overall outcome on a Bedrock Deal. The Power Plan is a top-down approach. It takes the measures that are used today and makes them a subset of the highest level.

In this example, which comes under Credibility in The Power Plan, the benchmark question is: 'Can we meet with the client CEO within seven days?' That is the engagement that needs to be established with credibility to win Bedrock Deals. You will need to meet with technical and legal and HR and marketing along your way to meeting with the CEO, so these questions don't need to be asked.

Put simply, the highest level you can establish within a methodology, the closer to the truth you arrive, the lower down you go, the more ticks you are likely to get; however, when you put all those ticks together, they mightn't affect the outcome, they won't tell you the truth. In saying this, I'm not advocating that current sales methodologies need to change. The Power Plan will overlay these sales methodologies by focusing what needs to be done back on the four core components of every deal: the 4C's.

The Power Plan brings a view to The Pursuit Plan for every deal that is actionable, forensic, disciplined, pragmatic and measurable. It takes the most important elements of the deal and essentially boils them down to four 'yes' or 'no' answers that can't be challenged. If there is one or more 'noes', then the right-to-win rating is close to 0.

We will now go into more detail on this starting with the first C:

1. Credibility

'Can we meet with the client CEO within seven days?'

The 'seven days' in this benchmark question is a nominal time frame to indicate whether the client CEO will see us when they're next available. This is the ultimate test of Credibility in The Bedrock Deal pursuit — remembering that a Bedrock Deal is one that is fundamental to the business operations of the client organisation. As such, the client CEO is the most important person in the deal pursuit, because the deal is important enough that they will likely have the final say on who wins it.

The answer to this benchmark question is black and white. It's either 'yes' or 'no'. A 'no' scores 0 for Credibility and your right to win The Bedrock Deal is 0. A 'yes' will be graded based on an adaptation of the equation I have used previously in this book:

$$Credibility = Knowledge \times Trust$$

We've discussed Knowledge previously in this book. Knowledge is having a solid understanding of the local, regional and global trends that affect the client organisation. It is a clear understanding of the strategic imperatives and the non-negotiables of the client organisation in relation to what they are going to achieve in the market, and how what you're selling relates back to these things.

This isn't as straightforward as it might sound, because it's very unlikely that what you're selling in itself will achieve the client's strategic imperative; instead, it will need to be fully explained relative to the strategic imperative, which requires a high degree of knowledge of the client, the solutions and the market. Knowledge is scored out of 10 and is ultimately determined by your message to the client CEO, which we'll cover in the sub-questions.

We've also discussed Trust earlier in this book. Trust is built when you deliver on the things that you have promised the client. This is most powerfully illustrated through the delivery of Stepping Stone Deals. Did your organisation deliver what your client expected in these deals to a high satisfaction level? If the answer is 'yes', then Trust has been built. Trust is scored out of 10 and is ultimately determined by client references, which we'll also cover in the sub-questions.

The first sub-question that applies if the answer to the Credibility benchmark question is 'no' is:

'What is the strategy to create credibility with the client CEO so they agree to meet us within seven days?'

Getting to meet the CEO is a stepping stone process. If you're working on a deal that is, say, four years out from closing and you've scored a 0 for Credibility, because the client CEO won't see you, then that's fine because you have plenty of time to build your Credibility within the client organisation.

To do this, the Client Expert and The Right Team should be actively talking to people in the client organisation. Talking to people in procurement, HR, product development, service delivery and so on. You might start down low in the client organisation. The same Credibility equation applies at this lower level. By talking to these people, you should be illustrating Knowledge and Trust to build Credibility.

Once you've established Credibility low down in the organisation, then you can move upwards. You can ask to see that person's boss and, because you're credible, that person will agree to arrange that meeting.

There is some risk if you start down low in the organisation that you will become 'gate kept' by that person. I've seen this happen many times. You need to avoid starting too low in the client organisation and avoid getting stuck there. This is where The Right Team can help. Because you have a range of talents and seniority in The Right Team, this can help you approach the client organisation at the right and different levels.

For example, your strategy to get a meeting with the client CEO might be to first get a meeting with the Head of Procurement. In that meeting, if you're talking about what your organisation does that directly relates to the client's strategic imperatives, then you're essentially talking the same language as the Head of Procurement. You're illustrating to them that you know what success looks like for that client organisation, which is the same message the Head of Procurement is receiving from the CEO.

The Head of Procurement will therefore know that you are invested in the success of the client organisation, and will be much more likely to agree to introduce you to the CEO because they know you will add value. They know you won't embarrass them in the meeting like many salespeople do today, by asking what the CEO did on the weekend or whether they like golf or whether they want to come to a client dinner. The Head of Procurement knows the meeting will be positive because you are speaking the same language as the client CEO and want to achieve the same outcomes.

You might find you'll need to meet with at least three or four heads of department to build Credibility before you ultimately get through to meet with the CEO. In this case, you would be replaying the same themes, just making them relevant to each department. This very much comes back to your call plan, which I will cover in the next chapter.

Conversely, your Trust in the client organisation might be high. You might have delivered everything you promised to a high level of client satisfaction over a decent period of time, but the CEO might not agree to see you. In this case, you might score Trust 8 but Knowledge is 0 (8 x 0 = 0). Your strategy here would be to learn that Knowledge.

The Client Expert and Sales Coach might need six months working on that Knowledge piece before they ask to see the CEO again. Alternatively, your organisation might be the undisputed expert in the solutions they deliver. You might score a 9 for Knowledge, but the CEO still won't agree to meet you, then Trust must be 0 (9 x 0 = 0).

In this case, Trust is a much harder thing than Knowledge to improve. It's easier to learn something than it is to change someone's opinion. If you're beginning a deal pursuit four years out in an industry new to your organisation, both your Knowledge and Trust scores may be

0 (0 x 0 = 0). In this case, you'd obviously need a strategy to improve both Knowledge and Trust, and you might not even try to get to see the client CEO until midway through the second year, when you know you've significantly improved both of these scores.

If the answer to the Credibility benchmark question is 'yes', then it needs to be graded based on one Knowledge sub-question and one Trust sub-question:

'What are our detailed contextualised messages to the client CEO?'

This is the Knowledge sub-question. What message can we deliver that adds the most value for the client CEO? As an organisation, we need to match what we do — and where and how we've done it — to the client's strategic imperatives to deliver a specific and relevant message for the client CEO. I say 'specific' because generic messages for any CEO are effectively meaningless.

The language to use here, which is the language of CEOs and senior executives, is 'implications'. This language must cover the facts in a 'if you do this, then this will happen' style. The messages should cover only a small number of points. The language needs to be targeted so it remains potent and doesn't get diluted. If you go in and try to sell everything at once, then it will become a generic conversation where the engagement from the CEO will be low.

The score for Knowledge is subjective and it will essentially come back to how well you know the client organisation and how good your messages are to them. Early on in the deal pursuit, you might be able to get a meeting with the CEO, but you might decide to wait a period of time to further build your Knowledge of the client to be able to deliver better and more targeted messages. You might only be able to score Knowledge after you've met the client CEO and asked validating questions during that meeting. Hopefully, in this case, you've done enough for the client CEO to invite you back.

'Has the client agreed to be a reference for another deal/client?'

This is the Trust sub-question. Does our client trust us enough to agree to act as a reference for another client? For example, your organisation might be working with a new retail organisation bidding for a first Stepping Stone Deal that you delivered to the existing client organisation six months earlier. Would the existing client CEO take a call from the CEO of this new retail organisation to tell them what your organisation is like? If the answer is 'yes', then the Trust score would be high because the existing client Trusts your organisation enough to endorse you to another organisation. Conversely, if the answer is 'no', then this score would be low and a Trust-building strategy would need to be put into place.

This sub-question also applies internally within the client organisation. For example, if you are meeting with someone a few levels below the CEO, has that person agreed to be a reference by introducing you to their boss so you can continue to work up the levels of the client organisation? This person, however, might falter by saying something like, 'Oh, I'm going on leave next week' or 'Can you come back and see me next week?' This clearly indicates that person doesn't trust you enough to make them look good, to sell a message to their boss that is consistent with the message from the client CEO. In this case, Trust = 0, which, regardless of your Knowledge score, means your Credibility is also 0.

This assumes that this person isn't a gatekeeper. You need to be aware of this scenario because it is common. To determine whether this person is a gatekeeper, you need to ask questions around what more you can do to get a meeting with their boss. It will fairly quickly become apparent, especially if you determine your Credibility is high yet you can't get that referral. You would then need to implement a strategy to get around this scenario, which would likely involve leveraging multiple relationships at the same time through The Right Team approach.

The score for Trust is subjective. Once derived, it is multiplied by the score for Knowledge to deliver an overall Credibility score out of 100. For example, if you score Knowledge 9 and Trust 8, then the Credibility score would be 72 (9 x 8 = 72).

2. Capability

'Do we have local reference sites that support our VantagePoint?'

This is the benchmark question for Capability. A local reference site for us in Australia is a reference site that delivers the same solution in the same industry segment within Australia as that of The Bedrock Deal. For example, a reference site in Melbourne in the banking and retail sector for cloud services, when The Bedrock Deal is in the banking sector for cloud services.

We've covered what a VantagePoint is. It's the statement that brings together the culture of the client you are pursuing, your own culture and the unique value you are bringing to that client into a 'we believe' statement.

A 'yes' answer to this benchmark question is a powerful indication to the client that you have the Capability to deliver The Bedrock Deal. It shows them you have gone through all the pitfalls and the problems associated with the rolling out of the solutions. It shows that you've invested in the right resources, team and capability to deliver those solutions. It shows you've got the partners in the back end to help with support. Ultimately, it demonstrates you have the entire ecosystem in place to deliver the solutions that are the requirements of The Bedrock Deal. Once again, this is a black-and-white 'yes' or 'no' answer. If the answer is 'no', then your Capability will score 0 and your right to win The Bedrock Deal is 0. A 'yes' will be graded based on this equation:

$$Capability = Competence \times Quantum$$

Competence measures your ability to deliver The Bedrock Deal. Competence is scored out of 10 and is ultimately determined by your local reference site(s) being in the top 5% of that client's service providers, which we'll cover in the sub-questions. Quantum is the number of local reference sites you have. Quantum is scored out of 10 and is ultimately determined by the broad base of references and/ or segmented reference capabilities you have, which we'll also cover in the sub-questions.

The first sub-question, which applies if the answer to the Capability benchmark question is 'no', is:

'What is the plan to introduce the client to relevant reference clients?'

Obviously, if you are pursuing a deal from a long way off and the answer to the benchmark question is 'no', then you have time to pursue a deal that will become your local reference site that supports your VantagePoint. You might find that you are delivering the same solutions locally in a different industry vertical. For example, you might be delivering the solution into the banking sector when The Bedrock Deal is in Government. In this case, you would need to come up with a plan to win a similar deal in Government within those four years.

You might also find, and I've seen this a number of times, where you are the incumbent and you've established a high enough level of Credibility with the client to be awarded a deal without a local reference site. For example, you might be delivering security to the client so well, that they accept this as the reference point, and award you the deal for customer applications. Obviously, you still need to go through the process and prove your capability in customer applications.

You can then use this deal as a local reference site for another client. This plan works. This illustrates the power of the first C: Credibility. There are many scenarios here, but obviously if the answer to the Capability benchmark question is 'no', then you must come up with a plan to turn it into a 'yes'. And if you're not a long way out from the deal — say, six months — and your Capability answer is 'no', then I would recommend walking away from that deal and concentrating your resources on your other deals.

This question also applies if the answer to the benchmark question is 'yes'. Obviously, if you have a local reference site that supports your VantagePoint with one client today, then you have to come up with a plan to get that CEO to meet with the CEO you're pursuing in an upcoming Bedrock Deal.

I have seen this plan overlooked many times. I've seen salespeople simply write down the reference site in the tender in a long-term pursuit without thinking about it further. The power of an existing client CEO recommending your organisation to a potential client CEO over a period of time is exceptional. Getting these CEOs together might involve inviting them to industry events, or hosting an executive dinner, or encouraging them to attend the company directors' association. There are many forums where this reference can be built over a period of time, but the plan needs to be put in place beyond simply putting a description of the reference in the formal tender process.

If the answer to the Capability benchmark question is 'yes', then it needs to be graded based on one Competence sub-question, followed by one Quantum sub-question:

'Is our reference site client rating us in their top 5% of their service providers?'

This is the Competence sub-question. The top 5% may sound high, but from my experience this is the level you achieve when you do what you say you were going to do with the right resources to deliver the outcomes the client expected. Further, if you're not in that top 5%, then your client probably doesn't view you as exceptional enough to want to recommend you to another client. In reality, you might get away with being in the top 10%, but for anything lower I'd argue the client views you as average. An average local reference site that supports your VantagePoint will obviously score low for Competence.

You might also need to do some work to determine whether your organisation is in your client's top 5%. Some organisations have a formal process of scoring their vendors, so in this case that score would be easily and objectively determined. If your client organisation doesn't have a process to score their vendors, then you might actually need to ask the question of the client CEO: 'Would you score my organisation in your top 5% of service providers?'

This may not be a day-one question, but one to ask when you've had significant experience with the client organisation. This is a really powerful question to ask a CEO because it will quickly uncover any issues you have. It's a far better question to ask then the usual: 'How are we doing?' or 'Do you have any complaints?' These are open-ended questions that lead to open-ended answers.

Asking the top 5% of service providers question is more subjective than receiving a score from those organisations that have a process to rate vendors, but you will still get your answer. You might also use The Right Team here to test out your score across a number of different people in different areas in the client organisation. The score for Competence hinges on whether you're in that top 5% of service providers. If you are, then your score out of 10 would be high, i.e. 7-10. If not, it would be low, i.e. <5.

'Do we have a broad base of references or segmented reference capabilities?'

This is the Quantum sub-question. Put simply, the broad base is the number of local reference sites you have that support your Vantage-Point. The more reference sites you have, the greater your score. For example, if you had, say, a dozen local reference sites, then your Quantum score would be high because essentially you can prove experience and delivery.

This can also be a very powerful competitive advantage. For example, if you have a number of sites you can rattle off and your competitor only has one. If you have only one or two local reference sites, then you might need to turn to segmented references.

A segmented reference is delivering different portions or parts of The Bedrock Deal to different clients that ultimately make up the whole. For example, you might have a local reference site for program management with one client, and project management with another client, and security with another client, and so on. And The Bedrock Deal includes all of these areas. You can therefore prove Capability across all of the services that need to be delivered, but not all at once to one client. A Capability score involving segmented references would score lower than having one local reference site for all of the services with one client.

The score for Quantum is subjective, but it is based on facts. You either have a number of reference sites or you do not. If you have 10 local reference sites, you might score Quantum 8. If you have one and a number of segmented reference capabilities, then your score might be a 3, and you might even be non-compliant. Once the score from Quantum is determined, it is multiplied by the score for Competence to determine the Capability Score out of 100.

Put simply, Capability is proving to the client that you can do what you say you can do. If the answer is 'no', then your right to win The Bedrock Deal is 0. If the answer is 'yes', then what is the strategy to illustrate this to the client? Can we illustrate that we've done it well? (That is, Are we Competent?) Can we illustrate that we've done it many times? (That is, do we have Quantum?)

If you have delivered it well and are in the top 5% of service providers, then you might score Competence 9. If you've delivered it 10 times, then you might also score Quantum 9. In this case, your Capability Score would be 81 (9 x 9 = 81).

3. Commitment

'Is the client currently buying from us?'

This is the Commitment benchmark question, and it is a pretty straightforward one. The premise here, which I have covered previously, is that it's very unlikely a client will trust another organisation to deliver a Bedrock Deal if they haven't done business with them before. Remembering a Bedrock Deal is one that fundamentally changes one of the client's business processes. Once again, the answer here is black and white. If the answer is 'no', then your score for Commitment is 0 and your right to win The Bedrock Deal is 0. A 'yes' will be graded based on this equation:

Commitment = Satisfaction x Outcome

Satisfaction is determined by asking how satisfied the client is with the services you are currently providing them. Satisfaction is scored out of 10 and is ultimately measured by the client, which we'll cover in the sub-questions. Outcome is the number of deals we have won with the client versus lost. Outcome is scored out of 10 and is ultimately determined by our 24-month win/loss ratio, which we'll also cover in the sub-questions.

The first sub-question, which applies if the answer to the Commitment benchmark question is 'no', is:

'What is our plan to gain a foothold in this client that supports our Bedrock Deal with complex services?'

This is where our Stepping Stone Deals in The Pursuit Plan come into play. What Stepping Stone Deals have the Client Expert and the Sales Coach identified in The Pursuit Plan in the lead-up to The Bedrock Deal? What strengths of our organisation are we going to leverage?

For example, our organisation might be excellent in security. The Bedrock Deal might not be a security deal, but we are going to win a number of Stepping Stone Deals in security with the client organisation to prove there's some Commitment to us from them. For example, we're going to enter the client organisation by doing a security assessment, then we're going to do some security consulting, then some training, and then some development of their policies and procedures, and so on. Winning all of these Stepping Stone Deals is designed to not only change the Commitment benchmark question from a 'no' into a 'yes', but to also improve our Satisfaction and Outcome scores along the way.

If the answer to the Commitment benchmark question is 'yes', then it needs to be graded based on one Satisfaction sub-question, followed by one Outcome sub-question:

'How satisfied is our client with our services?'

This is the Satisfaction sub-question and there are a number of mechanisms to measure client satisfaction out there today. I've spoken about The Net Promoter score in The Remuneration Plan, and how it's a great process that is poorly applied today. In addition, it needs to either be applied differently or another measure like an app-based approach needs to be put in place. If this can occur, then the score for client satisfaction will be objective. If not, then the score will be subjective and based on personal interactions with the client.

In this case, you'll need to be on your toes because there is a tendency in personal interactions for people to tell you what you want to hear. Ideally, you need to find a way to broaden these interactions throughout the organisation and give these people an anonymous way to give you this feedback, hopefully arriving at a fairly objective score out of 10 for Satisfaction.

'What is our 24-month win/loss deal ratio with the client?'

This is the Outcome sub-question. The measure here is pretty straightforward and the score is predominantly objective. The score out of 10 is equal to the same percentage as your win/loss deal ratio with that client over the last 24 months.

For example, if you went for six Stepping Stone Deals with the client and you won half of them, then your win/loss ratio is 3/6 or 50%, meaning your Outcome score is 5 (5/10 = 50%). This score assumes the deals all have equal weighting, which might not be the case, and is the reason why I say the score here is predominantly objective.

For example, if you won three product supply deals and lost three consulting deals, then that score would need to be subjectively modified because consulting deals are much more important to a client than product supply deals. In this case, although your win/loss ratio is 50%, you might downgrade your Outcome score from 5 to 3.

If you haven't won any Stepping Stone Deals in the last 24 months with the client, then obviously the score would be 0, and you should seriously consider whether to continue to pursue The Bedrock Deal with this client. As I've mentioned previously, in this case, you could heavily discount a Stepping Stone Deal to an irresistible level, just to determine once and for all whether the client will buy anything from you. If they don't buy that deal, then you need to walk away.

If your Outcome score is indeed 5, then to me that indicates that the client sees you as average. They are more than happy to share their business around. In this case, even if your score for Satisfaction is 10 (which seems unlikely if you're only winning 50% of the deals), you still wouldn't have a Commitment score of at least 60 (5 x 10 = 50). In this case, you'd need to come up with a strategy to improve that win/loss ratio and hopefully be far enough out from The Bedrock Deal to have the time to implement it.

Once the Outcome score is determined, it is multiplied by the Satisfaction score to determine the Commitment score out of 100. For example, if your Satisfaction score was 8 and your win/loss deal ratio over the last 24 months was 60%, i.e. 6, then your Commitment score would be 48 (8 x 6 = 48).

4. Control

'Are our fingerprints on the deal?'

This is the Control benchmark question. Fingerprints are a unique identifier. Every organisation has fingerprints: a set of unique skills and capabilities. I say a 'set' because it's not often an organisation has something intrinsically unique about itself, but those skills and capabilities can combine in a unique way.

Looking at the requirements in the tender, the Control benchmark question is asking: 'Has our organisation been able to Influence the client to include aspects in those requirements that are either unique to our organisation, or unique to a very small group of organisations?'

For example, in one organisation I worked for, we used to work really hard in big maintenance deals to get the client to include in the technical specifications a support for their end-of-life equipment. We did this because we knew that our biggest competitor wasn't able to deliver this, so they would be non-compliant on that requirement. When we were successful, our competitor knew it was us. They could see our fingerprints on the deal, and they would be very concerned at their likelihood of winning that deal, because they would have been doing everything they could to Influence the client out of including that requirement.

In this case, we were able to exert more Control over the deal than our competitor. The nuance here is that to gain Control you need to start early, i.e. one to two years out. If you start late, then you will run out of time. The other nuance is that you don't often know whether you've been successful in Controlling the deal until the tender comes out, which is quite late in the deal pursuit. That's the moment of truth with Control.

I'm not advocating that you need to establish Control over all the requirements of the deal. There might be 50 requirements and you might work hard on changing two or three of these requirements. These will be the requirements you're good at delivering, are unique to your organisation or a small number of organisations, and that you're well known for in the marketplace. This represents Control on up to 5% of the requirements of The Bedrock Deal. I've always said Bedrock Deals are a 1% game. You very rarely win a deal by more than that, so 5% is a significant competitive advantage.

On the flip side, if you have been working hard at changing those requirements over a significant period of time, and the tender comes to market without those changes, then the client is telling you they don't value you enough to include those changes. That's probably a sign that you haven't been able to build enough Credibility or prove Capability with that client. This is a worse outcome than coming late to a deal and running out of time. It basically tells you you've wasted all that time with the client. It also illustrates that the 4C's are inter-twined. You need Credibility and Capability to build Control.

I see a lot of salespeople today trying to talk their clients out of going to tender using a classic relationship strategy. They consider this the best approach: 'Let's be "clever", let's keep it under this value, let's contract doing this, come on, mate ....' In the end if it's a Bedrock Deal, it's always going to go to tender and, in this case, these salespeople have wasted the opportunity over all that time to Influence the deal.

For the most part, it is the best and most unique organisations that win Bedrock Deals, and if your salespeople aren't working on establishing those two things with the client, then they're wasting their time. Once again, the answer here is black and white. If the answer is 'no', then your score for Control is 0 and your right to win The Bedrock Deal is 0. A 'yes' will be graded based on this equation:

$$Control = Influence \times Mastery$$

Influence is: Have we been able to Influence the client to change their way of thinking towards our way of thinking? Influence is scored out of 10 and is ultimately measured by the level of your involvement in developing the client's strategy or aspects of the deal, which we'll cover in the sub-questions. Mastery is having a third party proving your expert credentials to the client. Mastery is scored out of 10 and is ultimately measured by the client demonstrating they recognise you to be an industry leader in the solution(s), which we'll cover in the sub-questions.

The first sub-question, which applies if the answer to the Control benchmark question is 'no', is:

'What are our next steps to create the control we need to achieve?'

If the tender comes out and you weren't able to exert any Control over it, then there are probably two reasons why.

Firstly, which I've mentioned, is that although you spent a significant amount of time with the client trying to shift their way of thinking towards yours, you failed. In this situation I would recommend not responding to the tender because this is a clear indication from the client that they don't value you enough to want to do business with you.

Secondly, which I've also mentioned, is that you were late to the tender and didn't have time to change the client's way of thinking towards yours. In this case, you might decide that because you have significant Credibility and/or Capability, it's worth having a go at the tender, but I guarantee you will be compromised somewhere in the deal.

Under The Right Model, The Pursuit Plan will ensure you will be talking to a client a long way out from the tender coming to market. Over this time, the Client Expert and the Sales Coach need to formulate and implement the strategy to establish Control. Initially, they will determine the requirements in the deal that are critical to the client that your organisation is an industry leader in (Mastery) and how to communicate this back to the client.

This could involve introducing a CEO from a local reference site where your Capability score is high in these requirements. You might brief that CEO to really emphasise you are the industry leader in those requirements. It could also be quoting an industry source that determines your organisation is an industry leader to the client.

There are a number of ways Mastery can be shown so that the client reflects this back to you. From there, the strategy would move towards Influence. How can we change the client's thinking about those requirements for them to include that change in the tender?

If the answer to the Control benchmark question is 'yes', then it needs to be graded, based on one Influence sub-question and one Mastery sub-question:

'Have we helped the client develop company and/or IT strategy and/or technical/commercial aspects of the deal?'

This is the Influence sub-question. It is basically asking: 'How engaged have we been with the client in relation to this tender, or generally, with their IT strategy?'

Under the banner of IT strategy, organisations have different architecture documents for different parts of their environments. For example: enterprise, security, cloud and so on. Clients generally get external organisations to either write or review these architecture documents. For example, if you have written the security architecture and reviewed the enterprise architecture for a client, then that is a high level of Influence because they obviously already value your organisation in those areas.

There's a caveat here. Sometimes when you do work 'above the line' on strategy, then this precludes you from working 'below the line', i.e. bidding on The Bedrock Deal related to that strategy. This isn't always the case, but, if it is, this will come back to the long-term strategy for the client. You might determine that the 'above the line' consulting deal might be worth $800K, but taking that might preclude you from the 'below the line' implementation deal, which might be worth many tens of millions. In this case, your choice here will come back to your Attainment Plan, which outlines your long-term strategy for that client.

The technical/commercial aspects of the deal we have spent some time on already. This comes back to whether you have been able to change the client's way of thinking on those aspects towards your way of thinking. A technical aspect is related to the solutions within the deal, whilst the commercial aspects are related to timing, payment terms, buy-back requirements and so on.

For example, with one Bedrock Deal that I was working on, we were able to convince the client to delay the tender by 12 months because we knew we had the right skilled resources coming free at this time. This allowed us to significantly lower our cost because there were no recruiting fees, and so on. It also gave us another 12 months to Influence the deal further. We were successful in winning this deal.

If you have managed to do this over one or more aspects alongside delivering IT strategy for that client, then your Influence score would be high. If you haven't managed to change one requirement of the deal and have worked on IT strategy with the client, then your score would be lower. The score for Influence is predominantly objective. Have we managed to Influence the client and to what extent?

To determine the score, a really clear lens needs to be applied to recognise what is one of your organisation's fingerprints and what is a generic requirement. I've seen salespeople try to claim a requirement as a fingerprint because it's something that their organisation was good at delivering. That would score low for Influence, say, 1, unless it was a requirement that you convinced the client to put in by changing their way of thinking, which would score, say, 8.

'What has the client done to demonstrate they recognise us as industry leaders in our solution space?'

This is the Mastery sub-question. The key here is that the client must recognise you as an industry leader. Every salesperson I know would walk into a client organisation and say they were the industry leader in such and such. That's a given. But how do we know the client believes us? The highest measure in this case would be a third party such as an industry publication like *Gartner* recognising this fact. The score for Mastery here is high because it can be presented like that: as a fact.

Another significant measure that I have mentioned is another client recommending you as an industry leader. This is a slightly lower measure than a respected industry publication. If your client doesn't care that you're an industry leader in a solution, then that solution isn't important to them. Mastery is only measured on the solutions your client sees as critical enough for them to want the best in the industry to deliver for them. And even if *Gartner* writes that you're the best in the industry, or another client recommends you as the best in the industry, the client still needs to reflect this back to you by implementing your ideas.

A high score for Mastery needs to be demonstrated by the client. If *Gartner* says you're the best in the industry and you have changed the client's approach to this solution, then your Mastery score will be high. If you don't have a third party to prove that you're an industry leader in the solutions you provide for a Bedrock Deal, then your Mastery score will be low.

And, really, this comes back to The CEO Sales Plan.

Put simply, if you're not industry leaders in some of the solutions you deliver in a Bedrock Deal, then, by extension, your ideas won't be the best; they will likely be generic and bland. They won't be unique enough to win that Bedrock Deal as a Right Deal with good margin and delivery, and so on.

In this case, your score for Mastery will be low alongside your right to win. If you are the industry leader in the solution that your client sees as critical, and they don't demonstrate this back to you by implementing your ideas, then your score for Mastery will also be low. In this case, you have the wrong client because they're either not striving to be the best they can be, or they're not listening to you, or they don't believe you. Or possibly you didn't push the client hard enough to acknowledge that what you're saying is important to them.

Sometimes you need to encourage the client to answer, 'Yes, that's right,' once you've outlined what is important to them. This should never be simply show and tell, you need to listen and encourage a healthy dialogue.

The score for Mastery, like Influence is predominantly objective. The client either demonstrates that they recognise you as the industry leader in some of the solutions you deliver, or they do not. Once the score for Mastery is determined, it is multiplied by the score for

Influence to deliver the Control score out of 100. For example, if the score for Influence was 8 and the score for Mastery was 10, then the Control score would be 80 (8 x 10 = 80).

Ultimately, Control comes down to whether you've been able to Influence the client to include aspects in the critical requirements of The Bedrock Deal that deliver you a competitive advantage, because that client sees you as the industry leader in those critical requirements. This sounds simple, but this requires you to not only change the client's thinking towards your own, but to be bloody good at what you do.

Your score for Control might not become entirely clear until quite late in the process when the tender comes to market, after you've already invested a lot of time and money in the process. You will, however, have a subjective indication of your Control score in the lead-up to the tender, and you would have already established the scores for the other 3C's.

*   *   *

Once all the scores for the 4C's have been determined, they need to be combined to determine the right-to-win score. To do this, simply add them together and divide by 4 to arrive at the right-to-win rating out of 100.

For example, if your Credibility score is 72, your Capability score 81, your Commitment score 48, and your Control score 80, then your overall right-to-win rating would be 71 (72+81+48+80 = 281, 281/4

= 70.25). This is also illustrated in the previous Power Plan Score diagram.

And just to reiterate: each Component score must be at least 60 and the combined or overall score must be at least 80 for an organisation to have a high right-to-win rating. A high right-to-win rating means the organisation is well positioned to win The Bedrock Deal.

11. The Call Plan

The Call Plan is critical to the implementation of The Pursuit and Power Plans, and is worth its own chapter.

The Pursuit Plan identifies when a meeting needs to take place with a client and the goals relative to The Power Plan (the 4C's) that need to be achieved. The Call Plan implements this strategy. It determines the structure of the meeting, the messages you need to deliver, how those messages relate back to which of the 4C's the meeting primarily relates to, whether another of the 4C's can be introduced, who's going to deliver those messages, and what the next steps will be.

I say 'which one of the 4C's the meeting primarily relates to', and I've mentioned this before, because every meeting must be targeted on only one or two things. If you try to cover everything at once, then the conversation becomes too generic and you don't receive the detailed insights you need to develop in the pursuit of Bedrock Deals.

The Call Plan is scored and that score flows back into The Pursuit Plan to help determine the next steps. If we use the analogy that The Pursuit Plan is a game of chess with The Bedrock Deal as the prize, then The Call Plan is one move in that game. The Call Plan determines how well that move went. The Pursuit Plan determines the next move. The Call Plan is critical to The Pursuit Plan because it provides structure.

For example, if The Pursuit Plan determines that the next move in the Pursuit concerns Credibility, and we have satisfied our benchmark question and can get to see the client CEO, then The Pursuit Plan will outline, say, the four most important factors to this CEO relative to their strategic imperatives. It will also outline our organisation's value proposition in relation to those four important factors, ultimately determining the things that need to be talked about in the meeting.

The Call Plan takes these components and puts them into a structure that can be rehearsed. This is an important part of The Call Plan. It enables the Sales Coach to coach all the participants in the meeting through role playing. To use a sporting analogy, a footballer trains six days a week and plays one day a week. That coaching ensures the footballer performs at the best of their ability on that one day. There is no difference here.

I've often heard salespeople say of a meeting with a client CEO today, 'We'll just wing it.' If I was the CEO of this salesperson, I would wonder what value they are adding to my organisation. I also believe that if I'm the CEO going to meet with a client CEO and I haven't been involved in any rehearsals, I would refuse to go to that meeting. I feel that strongly about it because we are talking about Bedrock Deals here, those big important deals that change the fundamental processes of the client organisation. These deals require maximum effort and a plan to win. Every meeting needs to move that deal forward. This is achieved by asking the client for something significant.

For example, would they like to see a local reference site, would they be a reference site for us, or would they introduce us to their boss, and so on. These are significant questions that move the deal forward. These are separate to asking them to go to an executive dinner, or to see us again. These asks aren't significant, as they don't move the deal forward.

Every meeting needs to be designed to increase your score relative to the 4C's. And every participant in the meeting needs to understand The Call Plan for the meeting and be involved in rehearsals for the meeting. These rehearsals don't need to be long, they can be half an hour. And once again, these are rehearsals for Bedrock Deals, not for every deal. And also once again, The Power Plan ensures you are only chasing those deals where you have a high right to win.

This might sound over the top to some of you, but let me put it this way. I've had feedback from clients in the past about colleagues, those relationship salespeople, who come in and want to talk about their weekend and sports and the weather. The client later tells me: 'Don't ever bring that person back in to see me because they wasted my time.'

Or these salespeople wax lyrical about their organisation's Net Promoter Score or staff awards. It seems to me every organisation out there has at some point announced that they have achieved a high score in both of these things. This needs to be raised only if it's relevant to the meeting, and only by pulling out what specifically it is in that award or score that actually helps this client and the conversation.

Or they come in and thank them for their business. Pleasantries and awards are always required, but the meeting should never mostly be about them. You must add value to increase your Power Plan score in every meeting. You must also test the assumptions you've made in The Pursuit Plan in meetings.

For example, if you're chasing the deal from a long way out and it's a new industry for your organisation, then The Right Team have probably made some assumptions around the client in terms of their competitive environment and what is important to them. The Call Plan enables these assumptions to be validated by the client. And there might be a dozen assumptions. The Call Plan will ensure all 12 are validated, not just one or two if you're 'winging it'. This ensures you will take the right path in your pursuit of the deal.

This is especially relevant when you consider that, due to time constraints today, the one-hour meeting often gets truncated into half an hour. The Call Plan ensures you can be that concise and tick off everything you need to achieve in the meeting. In the majority of cases, I recommend to all sellers today that a half-hour meeting is all that is needed. You must be able to get what you need across and learn what you need to learn within that time frame.

The Call Plan is owned by the Client Expert, with input from the Sales Coach. Everyone who is attending the meeting must also be involved. For example, if the Head of HR is attending the meeting, then they will contribute to The Call Plan and be involved in the rehearsals. The Sales Coach would moderate these rehearsals. The Sales Coach would very rarely attend a meeting in a Pursuit Plan. To use a sporting analogy, it is very rare for a coach to run onto the field of play.

The Call Plan is a document. It contains a number of elements that I would describe as general and others that I would describe as specific to the meeting. The general elements are straight out of The Pursuit Plan. These cover the client's beliefs, the client's strategic imperatives, the client's decision makers, the decision-making criteria, all of those elements that form the basis of The Pursuit Plan. These elements are important, but I call them general because they aren't likely to change between meetings and are only really relevant for any external participants in the meeting that need that background.

The specific elements relate specifically to the meeting. These cover a number of things. The first is 'Who is the person we're meeting with?' This isn't just their name and title. If they have an online profile, you should look them up well in advance of the meeting. You need to research if they're mentioned in any media articles, determining what memberships they have, and how long they have been with the company. All these things will help you to understand who they are.

For example, your conversation with them, if they've only been with the organisation for one month, is going to be a lot different to the one you would have if they've been with the organisation for five years or more. It's also important to know who else they have worked for. Were they working for a competitor? You'd then need to be sensitive to how you frame that competitor. Were they working for another client of yours? You'd then need to know how that other client views/values your organisation. All of these things are important to the content and context of your conversation in the meeting.

The second specific element is determining the message of the meeting and the method of scoring relative to which of the 4C's The Pursuit Plan has determined the meeting must address. For example, if you're three years out from the deal, then The Pursuit Plan may determine Capability is the best C to address because it's too early to meet with the CEO to further Credibility.

The meeting here might be with the Head of the area in which The Bedrock Deal sits and the goal might be to ascertain which requirements of the deal are most critical to them. Your strategy here would be to prove your Capability in a number of areas to determine which of those areas the client responds to best. This information can then be scored and fed back into The Pursuit Plan.

The third specific element is to hone the messages of the meeting. If you go into the meeting with a number of messages and rapid fire these at the client, they won't hear them as well as if they're wrapped into a story.

For example, using Capability as our C once more, the client might be a bank and you have a local reference site at another bank. You might begin by letting the client know you work with a number of banks in the region and that this bank is doing this, and that bank is doing that, and would that be of interest to you? Telling a much broader story in a conversational way, alongside inviting input from the client, rather than coming out and saying: 'Oh yeah, we do that with this bank over here. Would you like to come and have a look?'

These stories need to be rehearsed. If you have three or four stories like this in your back pocket in the meeting, then it allows you to guide the meeting and not have to worry about each individual message. Once you tell these stories, you can build those individual messages out from there. And there are plenty of good books out there that can help with storytelling in detail, such as *Stories For Work: The Essential Guide to Business Storytelling* by Gabrielle Dolan.

The fourth and last specific element of The Call Plan is that it delivers a one-page summary that can be used in the meeting to tick off everything you've determined needs to be covered.

Once the meeting has taken place The Call Plan scores the outcomes, generates next steps and assigns owners to these steps. For example, using the Capability example above, the defined meeting outcome was to introduce a reference site to the client that they want/agree to attend. We told a number of stories around reference sites and we achieved the intended outcome. We asked the client that significant question and they said 'yes'. The score here would be high: 10/10.

The next step would be to contact the preordained CEO or CIO at that reference site to organise the visit. The owner of this step would be identified and a due date determined. All these outcomes would then be fed back into The Pursuit Plan. It would also ensure that you can review and recap with the client the outcomes of the last meeting in your next meeting. This is really important because it enables you to reset the baseline. It enables you to determine that what was important to the client at the last meeting is still important to them now, because this can change.

The vast majority of meetings I've attended without Call Plans end without any measurable movement towards winning the deal, and often end with what I call 'happy clapping'. 'Please come back and see me anytime. Oh, you're in town next month, sure, look me up.' I call this 'happy clapping' because everyone's happy, but ultimately the meeting achieved nothing and the result is let's have another 'happy clap' later. From my experience, often the client is agreeing to another meeting just to get you out the door and they will come up with excuses not to see you again.

The Call Plan ensures you get a lot more out of the meeting than just another meeting. The Call Plan moves the deal forward by ensuring every meeting addresses desired outcomes related to one of the 4C's as determined by The Pursuit Plan. If these outcomes are achieved, then this increases your Power Plan score which, in turn, increases your right to win The Bedrock Deal. One step forward rather than another step sideways, or backwards.

12. Implementation of The Right Model

How Long Will It Take to Fully Implement The Right Model?

The Right Model is not a quick fix. It is a significant restructure of your organisation, turning it to face your clients. It ensures your organisation is more informed and proactive to your clients' needs and outcomes.

The Right Model would be implemented in stages. It would begin with you, the CEO, completing The CEO Sales Plan. I estimate this plan would take two to three months to complete and a total of 12 months to implement. Remember: this is a detailed analysis of where your market's going, where you want your market to go, who your clients are and where they're headed, which clients you may need to transition out of, and which clients you now need to go and pursue to transition into your future. It is the strategy document that guides your organisation over the next five years.

Whilst The CEO Sales Plan is being implemented, The Team Plan and The Remuneration Plan can commence. If we think about the three elements to The Right Model (Clients, Team and Deals), then The CEO Sales Plan will outline The Right Clients and The Right Deals whilst work on The Right Team can begin. The Team Plan will start skilling your organisation up for The Right Model. The Remuneration Plan will ensure they will be focused as a team.

As I've said previously, this might involve running a two-phase sales team for some time, maybe even a couple of years. This ensures you have the personnel in place to protect the current deals, whilst introducing your Sales Coach and Client Experts to these and the new deals. You won't be adding head count but transitioning some staff, whilst replacing those that leave through natural attrition. The secret here is that we want to transition current staff and protect the business by delivering the agreed numbers.

The Pursuit and Power Plans can also be implemented whilst The CEO Sales Plan is being implemented. By running The Power Plan over your pipeline, you will better understand your business. You will be able to throw deals out of the pipeline that you have no chance of winning, whilst replacing them with deals that you have a high right to win. These deals can then be put into a Pursuit Plan without any significant structural change to the organisation. This analysis can then be fed back into The CEO Sales Plan.

Once The CEO Sales Plan has been completed, the last piece of The Right Model, The Attainment Plan, can then be put into place. This is likely to be at the one-year mark. So the first year is spent predominantly on implementation. The second year would consolidate that implementation, alongside realising The CEO Sales Plan through The Attainment Plan. Year two would also require an absolutely dedicated and focused discipline to ensure that the elements of The Right Model begin to generate themselves. Year three would involve further consolidation and fine tuning. Year four would realise the results.

To use a sporting analogy:

- Year one is spent on coming up with the team structures and roles that ensure the team to play the way the coach has decided they want the team to play.

- The second year is spent learning that structure and the roles to ensure they become instinctive to the team.

- Year three is spent fine-tuning the structure and roles.

- Year four will realise the end result of all these changes.

The same is true of The Right Model. From day one of deciding to go down this path, I'd imagine it would be a three- to four-year process for it to be fully realised.

As a CEO, there will be two major challenges along the way. The first involves the short and long game balance, i.e. continuing to deliver the numbers whilst transitioning to a new model. I'd argue that this is little different from the challenges a CEO faces today. The numbers are always a challenge and the marketplace and organisation are always in flux.

The second major challenge is ensuring that your executive, sales and solutions teams are on-board with the changes. This will require, from your people leader, a significant organisational change-management strategy. Once again, in an environment where change is the norm, this challenge is one that faces many CEOs today and every day. I'd argue that every organisation today has a change-management strategy in place to manage their day-to-day. This is business as usual for most CEOs. The other smaller challenges around keeping the market informed, and educating your clients and partners on these changes, are also things most CEOs are already doing today.

As a CEO, you should begin to see changes in the first month The Right Model is implemented. The Power Plan will very quickly change your pipeline, removing those deals that have a low right-to-win score, leaving those deals where the right-to-win score is highest. This will no doubt initially create some awkward moments with the sales team, but, as the CEO, you must stay the course. Over time this awkwardness will dissipate because, as the role model, your sales team will begin to follow you.

Alternatively, there might be deals in the pipeline where the right to win is low, and, by running The Power Plan over those deals, you might determine that they are salvageable. The Power Plan will identify the gaps that need to be filled by The Pursuit Plan for that deal to move towards a high right-to-win score.

Essentially, you will see more and more of these high right-to-win deals emerging in the pipeline, over time, to create a robust and defendable pipeline. That's not to say the revenue will flow immediately, as these Bedrock Deals in the pipeline will likely be at least six to twelve months off, but an increase in confidence about the future will emerge early on in the implementation of The Right Model.

The other change you should begin to see when The Right Model is implemented is that the rift between the current salespeople and the departments around them begins to mend. You will begin to see a culture that embraces the team, rather than the individual. This will lead to better communication within the organisation, a better understanding across the business of what it takes to win deals, and a willingness in the organisation to go that extra mile to win a deal.

What Does The Right Model Look Like from Inside the Organisation?

The Right Model not only ensures a robust and reliable pipeline, but it will change the shape of the pipeline as we know it today. The Right Model pipeline will significantly grow the pipeline of today between the three- to five-year period, whilst reducing it in the one- to two-year period. This will be achieved because The Pursuit Plan can better enable those long-term deal pursuits, whilst The Power Plan will ensure you are only working on those deals where you have a high right to win and which are closing in under two years.

Here's a graphical representation of The Right Model Pipeline versus the Traditional Pipeline:

PIPELINE COMPARISON 10 MIL TARGET

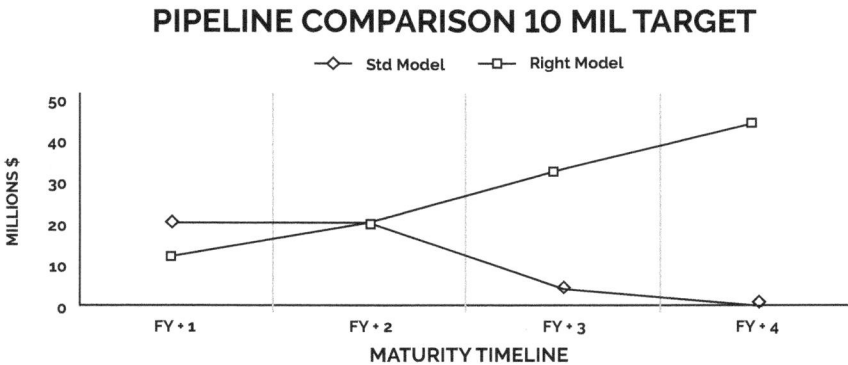

The Right Model also ensures that everybody in your organisation has a better understanding of each Bedrock Deal. As a CEO, you will be able to walk up to a number of people in your organisation involved in a Bedrock Deal and have a meaningful conversation about it. You will also see that your client engagement goes up significantly because the processes in The Pursuit Plan ensure that your Client Experts are exactly that: experts on your clients.

You will also see your organisation working together as a team because your people are remunerated on company success, not individual success. You will also see greater involvement from your partners, because your Client Experts have a greater understanding of their clients than what your partners' other partners have. You will hear fewer conversations about tactical discounting. You will see your staff turnover fall. You will also see an organisation that is committed to helping their clients change, as opposed to just addressing minor business problems with them.

What Does The Right Model Look Like from Outside the Organisation?

Clients and partners will see Client Experts who are significantly more focused than the traditional salesperson of today. They will see Client Experts who know what their organisation can do, and, more importantly, what they can't do. They will see an urgency from Client Experts delivering more outcomes with less activity. They will also see the same Client Experts year after year after year, because The Right Model creates a truly collaborative and enjoyable organisation to work for. It's not simply a couple of signs hanging on the wall that say something like:

1. Our staff are our most important asset

and

2. Our clients are at the centre of everything we do.

It's a model that delivers on these claims.

Is The Right Model Right for My Organisation?

Now it's time to apply the changes to your business that The Right Model will create in order to see if the returns justify the effort required to implement it.

The What's It Costing You 'back of the coaster equation' below will help you to do this.

The basis of The What's It Costing You 'back of the coaster equation' is built from the six areas in your organisation that I believe — when using a traditional sales model — are costing your organisation money through inefficiency. I've estimated a percentage in each of these six areas. The exact percentages may vary in your organisation, but by using this diagram as a guide, you will be able to estimate what the cost of your current sales set-up is to your bottom line.

What's it costing you?

Sales Recruitment
Hubspot says that sales team turnover is sitting at 35% coupled with our figure of a 25% waste in your sales budget. We estimate you are wasting 20% of your recruitment budget in failed sales hires.
Your Cost = ...$

Sales Engine
Our experience shows that 30% of a sales team do not sell anything in a set year, while of the remaining sales team members only 20% meet or exceed their target. Taking into account environmental circumstances we estimate this is a waste of 25% of your sales budget.
Your Cost = ...$

Marketing Effort
Most research shows that approximately 50% of your marketing budget is wasted. We estimate that 15% of the total waste is directly attributed to your Sales Engine.
Your Cost = ...$

Sales Support Teams
We estimate that 10% of your Sales Support Team's effort is being wasted on unproductive tasks driven by your Sales Engine.
Your Cost = ...$

Pre-Sales Engine
With lack of strategy and detailed client engagements leading to the pursuit of poorly qualified deals we estimate that 20% of your presales budget is wasted.
Your Cost = ...$

Legal and Professional
We estimate that poorly qualified deals are costing organisations in legal and professional fees 10% of the budget.
Your Cost = ...$

Your Total Cost = $

By implementing The Right Model, I believe all six of these costs will be greatly reduced in your organisation, and be flowing instead as margin through to the bottom line.

Of course, this estimate is simply a quick check, but if the costs are substantial, then a more significant investment in a more robust review is warranted. Please contact the CEO-Led Sales Team for more information:

www.ceoledsales.com.au

Conclusion

If you've read this far, then I thank you for staying the course and I hope you got a lot out of this book.

I speak to a lot of colleagues in the IT industry today who know the sales approach is broken, but they're resigned to this fact and they do everything they can with this broken system to make it work. I've been there myself.

The market is constantly evolving and I believe a point will be reached, in the not-too-distant future, where organisations that don't change their sales approach will struggle to survive. I truly believe there is a better approach out there that will ensure organisations survive and thrive into the future.

This change of approach starts at the top, with you: the CEO. If you're sick of fast-talking sales managers, slippery pipelines and the pressure to win that last-minute deal, then you need The Right Model. I promise you that once you begin, you won't regret it.

Acknowledgments

If embarking upon the crazy journey of writing a book, everyone needs a Chris Grierson and Andrew Ford in their life. Andrew and Chris kept this project on track, were full of fresh ideas, cracked the whip when needed, always complimented my beer-making skills, and are two great blokes; without them, you would be holding fresh air right now.

Thank you for the exceptional proofreads, Shona Deforest and Clair Hawck. The time and effort you took to read, review, comment and delicately spare my feelings were truly appreciated; fitting this extra workload into your schedules was also amazing.

I asked Dave D'Aprano if he would consider writing the foreword to this book early in 2019. He readily accepted, then became used to me delaying the date that he would receive the manuscript. If this book were a Bedrock Deal, in the forecast, it would have been the bane of any sales leader — thanks for your patience and immense experience in reviewing this book, Dave.

Upon joining the enterprise-selling community, and becoming familiar with juggling the demands of $100+ million deals, I met and was educated by some exceptional and talented people. Scott Whyman took the risk and hired me into the IT Industry at Unisys, giving me an opportunity with no previous enterprise-selling roles, or any role in IT. John Preller for coaching me with interview skills for that first job at Unisys and for still being very generous with his time today to help me refine ideas. Christine Carey, Peter Whitely, Michael Vandenheide, and Kevin McIsaac taught me about the importance of demanding excellence, living your customer outcomes, collaborating with your customer, and thinking globally. Later in my career, I was influenced greatly by Ken Westwood, James Penton, Grant Hawksworth, Danny Gorup, Greg Thomas, Lysandra Schmutter, Sven Brook and David Milo — you wonderful people exude strategy, technical wisdom and broad business sense. Your approach, while different from each other, is always focused on an excellent outcome for your clients.

In the depths of writing the book, I needed some technical help. Tim McElwaine, Gavin Dudley, David Bird, Mark Turner, Michelle Ridsdale, and Michelle Hart freely took phone calls, reviewed and made detailed and insightful suggestions, driving significant improvements in the manuscript. Thank you very much.

I've got some great mates: Dale Brown, John Anderson, Shane Connolly, Keith Tomlin, Jeff Lipscombe, Paul Lewis, Peta Swarbrick, Steve Horswell, Brenton Hawck and Marty Przybylak. You have all grown to tolerate my sometimes erratic approach to the world and my constant urging to 'come ride the Simpson Desert with me', but most of all you have been continuously there, a number of you for over 40 years, keeping me honest and grounded. Thank you.

About The Author

Andrew Phillips is a dynamic executive leader with extensive experience in the contemporary management of people and projects. He demonstrates an ability to consistently deliver outstanding value and profitable growth for both corporate and government organisations.

With a background in business consulting, spanning 30 years, Andrew is a senior sales professional, business analyst and project manager with an impressive track record delivering value propositions and change agendas.

Honest, outcome-orientated and intensely passionate about providing constructive support to his team, Andrew provides inspirational leadership by setting a clear vision and driving a culture of excellence. With an innate ability to identify and diagnose business technology problems, create scalable and profitable solutions for his clients, Andrew has earned a reputation as a trusted advisor, integral to his clients' overall business strategies.

Widely recognised as a thought leader, Andrew has provided strategic guidance to CEOs and organisations, including Unisys, Nortel, Meta Group, Getronics, Dimension Data and Readify. Andrew is recognised as a leader in his field and one of the most sought-after sales professionals in Australia.

Author of *CEO-Led Sales*, Andrew begins a new chapter of his career, focusing his energy on helping CEOs transform their organisations into dependable and consistent revenue generators.